Nelson *Mathematics* 3

Teacher's Resource

Chapter 12: Fractions

Series Authors and Senior Consultants
Marian Small • Mary Lou Kestell

Senior Authors
Heather Kelleher • Kathy Kubota-Zarivnij • Pal Milol
Betty Morris • Doug Super

Teacher's Resource Chapter Author
Wendy Klassen

Assessment Consultant
Damian Cooper

THOMSON

NELSON

Australia   Canada   Mexico   Singapore   Spain   United Kingdom   United States

THOMSON

NELSON

Nelson Mathematics 3
Teacher's Resource

Series Authors and
Senior Consultants
Marian Small, Mary Lou Kestell

Senior Authors
Heather Kelleher,
Kathy Kubota-Zarivnij, Pat Milot,
Betty Morris, Doug Super

Authors
Carole Adam, Anne Cirillo,
Jennifer Brown, Jack Hope,
Wendy Klassen, Joanne Languay,
Marian Small, Ian Stackhouse,
Susan Stuart, Stella Tossell

Assessment Consultant
Damian Cooper

Director of Publishing
David Steele

Publisher, Mathematics
Beverley Buxton

Senior Program Manager
Shirley Barrett

Teacher's Resource
Program Managers
Alan Simpson
David Spiegel

Developmental Editors
Janis Barr
Julie Bedford
Jenna Dunlop
Anna Garnham
James Gladstone
Adrienne Mason
Margaret McClintock
Janice Nixon
Frances Purslow
Elizabeth Salomons
Tom Shields
Alan Simpson
Michael Tabor

Editorial Assistant
Megan Robinson

Executive Managing Editor,
Development & Testing
Cheryl Turner

Executive Managing Editor,
Production
Nicola Balfour

Senior Production Editor
Linh Vu

Copy Editor
Linda Szostak

Senior Production Coordinator
Sharon Latta Paterson

Production Coordinator
Franca Mandarino

Creative Director
Angela Cluer

Art Director
Ken Phipps

Art Management
ArtPlus Ltd., Suzanne Peden

Illustrators
ArtPlus Ltd.

Interior and Cover Design
Suzanne Peden

Cover Image
T. Kitchin/First Light

ArtPlus Ltd. Production
Coordinator
Dana Lloyd

Composition
Valerie Bateman/ArtPlus Ltd.

Photo Research and
Permissions
Vicki Gould

Printer
Frisby Litho

National Library of Canada
Cataloguing in Publication

Nelson mathematics 3.
Teacher's resource / Marian Small ...
[et al.].

ISBN 0-17-620094-0

1. Mathematics—Study and
teaching (Primary)
I. Small, Marian
II. Title: Nelson mathematics three.

QA135.6.N443 2003 Suppl. 3
510   C2003-904834-9

Contents

Introduction

This chapter extends students' fraction knowledge from Grade 2 by

- extending their ability to identify and compare fractions using concrete materials to doing so pictorially and symbolically
- extending their understanding of fractions beyond fractions as parts of a whole, to fractions as parts of a set and as parts of a measure
- using more precise vocabulary to describe fractions and mixed numbers

While the emphasis at this level remains on the concrete, the connection is made to pictures and symbols. As well, a focus is placed on communicating: representing and explaining fractions using drawings.

Communication Focus: Describing Fractions

Lesson 3 focuses on the importance of communicating with sufficient detail, including in the text and with drawings, in the context of writing instructions.

Curriculum Across Grades 2 to 4: Fractions

All the Grade 3 expectations listed below are covered in this chapter.
When the expectation is a focus of the lesson, the lesson number is indicated in brackets.

Grade 2	Grade 3	Grade 4
Overall Expectations: Number Sense and Numeration • compare proper fractions using concrete materials	**Overall Expectations: Number Sense and Numeration** • represent common fractions and mixed numbers using concrete materials **(1, 2, 3, 4, 5)** • solve problems and describe and explain the variety of strategies used **(4)**	**Overall Expectations: Number Sense and Numeration** • compare and order mixed numbers and proper and improper fractions with like denominators using concrete materials and drawings • represent and explore the relationships between decimals, mixed numbers, and fractions using concrete materials and drawings
Specific Expectations: Understanding Number • represent and explain halves, thirds, and quarters as part of a whole and as part of a set using concrete materials and drawings • compare two proper fractions using concrete materials	**Specific Expectations: Understanding Number** • represent and explain common fractions, presented in real-life situations, as part of a whole, part of a set, and part of a measure using concrete materials and drawings **(1, 2, 3, 4)**	**Specific Expectations: Understanding Number** • represent, compare, and order mixed numbers and proper and improper fractions with like denominators using concrete materials and drawings • connect proper fractions with decimals (tenths and hundredths) using concrete materials, drawings, and symbols • explore the relationships between fractions and decimals using a calculator, concrete materials, and drawings

Math Background: Research and Important Issues

Students will have had experience using concrete materials to compare fractions as parts of wholes. They continue to do that in this chapter. Regular geometric regions are used as fraction models.

Fractions as Parts of a Whole: Whole units are easily represented using pattern blocks, and fractions or parts of wholes can be shown with other pattern blocks. Students should have practice manipulating the blocks to show fractions. Students should then connect those manipulations to pictures, determining if a region has been divided into equal parts and naming the parts as fractions. This connection should ultimately relate the symbolic form of the fraction to the concrete materials and the pictures. Fractions as parts of wholes will be represented with a variety of polygons and circles in this chapter.

Fractions as Parts of a Group (Set): At the simplest stage, students identify the number within a set that has a certain characteristic. That number over the total number of the set is the fraction of the set. For example, if 3 counters out of 10 are red, the red counters make up $\frac{3}{10}$ of the entire set of counters.

Fractions as Parts of Measurement: The measurement model of fractions is similar to the concept of fractions as part of a whole. Measurement is continuous—the units are all joined together to make a whole. The unit being measured, whether it be a unit of time, length, capacity, or some other measure, is considered the whole, and the parts of the whole are the fractions of the measure. So, for example, if a length of ribbon was the unit and it was folded into four parts, each part would be $\frac{1}{4}$ of the total length.

Mixed Numbers: A mixed number is a number made up of a whole number and a fraction. The important concept for students to understand when making, finding, or reading mixed numbers is that one whole is made up of all of the parts of a given set or region of measurement. That is, if the region is divided into six parts, the whole region is equal to $\frac{6}{6}$ or all of the parts.

Planning for Instruction

Problem Solving

- Assign a Problem of the Week each week from the selection below (see sample answers on p. 60) or from your own collection.
  1. Look at the main buttons on a telephone pad.
     - What fraction of the buttons has
       - letters
       - an odd number
       - a P
       - a vowel
       - a letter in the word "math"
       - no numbers
  2. Look at a map of Canada to find its 10 provinces.
     - What fraction describes the provinces that
       - are west of Ontario
       - have a name starting with N
     - What could you say about $\frac{1}{5}$ of the provinces?
     - Make up two fraction questions about the provinces.
  3.
     - Draw pictures of coins to show how you can have $\frac{4}{10}$ of a dime. Circle the coins that show $\frac{4}{10}$.
     - Draw pictures of coins to show how you can have $\frac{4}{10}$ of a dollar. Circle the coins that show $\frac{4}{10}$.
     - Did you use the same number of coins?
     - Can you use a different number of coins to show $\frac{4}{10}$ of a dollar? Explain.

Connections to Literature

Add books to your classroom that are related to the math in this chapter. For example:

A Giraffe and a Half (Shel Silverstein; Harper & Row, 1964)

Eating Fractions (Bruce McMillan; Scholastic, 1991)

Ed Emberley's Picture Pie (Ed Emberley; Little Brown & Company, 1984)

Gator Pie (Louise Mathews; Dodd Mead, 1979)

Ten for Dinner (JoEllen Bogart; Scholastic, 1989)

The Hershey's Milk Chocolate Fractions (Jerry Pallota; Scholastic, Cartwheel Books, 1999)

Connections to Other Math Strands

Measurement: Have students look through flyers and newspapers to discover sales. Students can investigate what would happen to the price of a $24 item if it was on sale for $\frac{1}{3}$ off, or $\frac{1}{4}$ off, or $\frac{1}{2}$ off.

Students can explore the relationships among coins. For example, a penny is $\frac{1}{5}$ of a nickel; a penny is $\frac{1}{10}$ of a dime; a nickel is $\frac{1}{2}$ a dime; a dime is $\frac{1}{10}$ of a loonie, and so on.

Geometry: As students work with pattern blocks, they can start to discover relationships between 2-D shapes. (For example, $\frac{1}{2}$ of a rhombus is a triangle, $\frac{1}{6}$ of a hexagon is a triangle, and so on.)

Connections to Other Curricula

Music: Talk with the students about the symbols for, and the meanings of, quarter, half, and whole notes. Reinforce these fractional concepts as you read through a piece of music together. Make clear the understanding that the beats in each bar in a piece of music must equal the same amount, and for those students who are knowledgeable about music, you may want to discuss the time signature. Encourage students to write their own music using a variety of notes.

Physical Education: Many gymnastics and dance moves require moving $\frac{1}{4}$ turns, $\frac{1}{2}$ turns, and full turns along with directions. These relate to fractions of a circle. For example, in a line dance, students might be asked to lift their knee, turn $\frac{1}{4}$ to the left, and stomp their heel and toe. When students follow or create a gymnastic or dance routine, have them describe to the class some of the moves using fractions.

Connections to Home and Community

- Send home the Family Newsletter (Master on p. 45).
- Have students complete the *Math 3 Workbook* pages for this chapter at home.
- Use the At Home suggestions found in most lessons.

Chapter 12 Planning Chart

Key Concepts

Numbers tell how many or how much.

Classifying numbers provides information about the characteristics and meaning of numbers.

There are different, but equivalent, representations for a number.

Chapter Goals

Represent and describe fractions.

Use diagrams to communicate about fractions.

Represent and describe mixed fractions.

Student Book Section	Lesson Goal	ON Expectation	Pacing 9 days	Prerequisite Skills/Concepts
Getting Started: Common Fractions, pp. 286–287 (TR pp. 10–12)	Use concepts and skills developed prior to this chapter.		1 day	• Compare proper fractions using concrete materials. • Represent and explain halves, thirds, and quarters as parts of a whole and parts of a set using concrete materials and drawings.
Lesson 1: Guided Activity Fractions as Parts of a Group, pp. 288–289 (TR pp. 13–16)	Use fractions to describe parts of a group.	3m3, 3m20	1 day	• Represent and explain halves, thirds, and quarters as part of a set using concrete materials.
Lesson 2: Guided Activity Fractions as Parts of a Whole, pp. 290–291 (TR pp. 17–20)	Use fractions to describe parts of a whole.	3m3, 3m20	1 day	• Represent and explain halves, thirds, and quarters as part of a whole using concrete materials.
Lesson 3: Guided Activity Communicate Using Drawings, pp. 292–293 (TR pp. 21–24)	Represent and explain fractions using drawings.	3m3, 3m20	1 day	• Recognize fractions as parts of wholes.
Lesson 4: Exploration Fractions as Parts of a Measure, p. 296 (TR pp. 29–31)	Use fractions to describe parts of a measure.	3m3, 3m8, 3m20	1 day	• Represent proper fractions using concrete materials.
Lesson 5: Direct Instruction Mixed Numbers, pp. 298–299 (TR pp. 33–36)	Model and describe mixed numbers.	3m3	1 day	• Represent proper fractions using concrete materials and drawings.
Mid-Chapter Review: p. 294 (TR pp. 25–27) **Math Game:** p. 295 (TR p. 28) **Curious Math:** p. 297 (TR p. 32) **Mental Imagery:** p. 300 (TR p. 37) **Skills Bank:** pp. 301–302 (TR p. 38) **Problem Bank:** p. 303 (TR p. 39) **Chapter Review:** pp. 304–305 (TR pp. 40–42) **Chapter Task:** p. 306 (TR pp. 43–44)			3 days	

Materials	Masters/Workbook	Extra Practice and Extension in the Student Book
2-coloured counters, 4/student	(for Extra Support) Scaffolding p. 52 (for Extra Support) Scaffolding p. 53 Fraction Mats p. 59 (for Assessment) Initial Assessment Summary, p. 1	
2-coloured counters, 10/student (for Extra Challenge) red and white blocks	Mental Math p. 46 (for Extra Support of Questions 6 & 7) Scaffolding p. 54 Workbook p. 92	Mid-Chapter Review Questions 1 & 2 Skills Bank Questions 1 & 2 Problem Bank Questions 1, 2, & 3 Chapter Review Questions 1, 2, & 3
pencil crayons pattern blocks	Mental Math p. 46 (for Extra Support of Question 6) Scaffolding p. 55 Fraction Mats p. 59 (manipulatives substitute) Pattern Blocks, Masters Booklet pp. 40, 42, 44, 45 Workbook p. 93	Mid-Chapter Review Questions 3, 4, 5, & 6 Skills Bank Questions 3, 4, & 5 Problem Bank Questions 4 & 5 Chapter Review Questions 4, 5, & 6
scissors, 1 pair/student (optional) cans (optional) paper circle, paper rectangle, paper square, 1 each/student	Mental Math p. 47 Workbook p. 94	Chapter Review Question 7
ribbon or strip of paper, 1 piece/student glass and water, 1/group a clock with movable hands, 1/group (optional) calendar, a ruler, a metre stick, various sizes of containers	Mental Math p. 47 (for Assessment) Problem-Solving Rubric, Masters Booklet p. 7 Workbook p. 95	Skills Bank Questions 6 & 7 Problem Bank Question 6 Chapter Review Questions 8 & 9
pattern blocks: hexagon, trapezoid, rhombus, triangle (for Extra Support) paper squares	Mental Math p. 47 (for Extra Support of Questions 6, 7, & 8) Scaffolding p. 56 (manipulatives substitute) Pattern Blocks, Masters Booklet pp. 40, 42, 44, 45 Workbook p. 96	Skills Bank Questions 8 & 9 Chapter Review Question 10
2-coloured counters scissors geoboards pattern blocks (optional) balance scales, large ball of clay (optional) coins (pennies, dimes, nickels), (optional) paper strips (optional) ribbon	Chapter 12 Test Pages 1 & 2, pp. 48–49 Chapter Task Pages 1 & 2, pp. 50–51 Fraction Concentration Cards pp. 57–58 Fraction Mats p. 59 2 cm Square Dot Paper, Masters Booklet p. 26 (manipulatives substitute) Play Money 1, Masters Booklet p. 28 Workbook p. 97	

Planning for Assessment

The Chapter 12 Assessment Chart on the next page lists many opportunities for assessment using a variety of strategies: skills demonstration, short answers, written questions, investigation, observation, and product making. To guide you, refer to the recording tools and samples provided in the Masters Booklet pages 1 to 16.

Managing Initial Assessment

- To see the specific assessment suggestions for Getting Started, refer to pages 10 to 12 in this booklet. This initial assessment opportunity includes the activity Common Fractions, and three skills-based questions in Do You Remember?
- You may use other initial assessments involving informal interviews or written questions (for example, your own diagnostic activity).
- Use *Initial Assessment Summary* (Tool 1) to help you record your observations and concerns about the prior knowledge that an individual brings to Chapter 12. You may choose to record observations for all students, or for only those individuals who appear to have difficulty.

Managing Assessment for Feedback

- To see the specific assessment suggestions for Lessons 1 to 5, refer to the second column of the Chapter 12 Assessment Chart on the next page.
- You may use other informal feedback assessments involving ongoing observations and interviews to help you adapt your instruction to suit individual students' needs.
- Use any of these instructions and tools to help you improve student achievement:
  What to Look for When Assessing Student Achievement (Tool 2)
  Coaching Students Toward Success (Tool 3)
  Conducting In-Class Student Interviews
  Student Interview Form (with prompts) (Tool 4)
  Student Interview Form (without prompts) (Tool 5)
- **Peer Assessment:** As students are working together, encourage them to listen to one another and assist if appropriate. Good opportunities for informal peer assessment occur in Exploration Lesson 4, Communication Lesson 3, and the Math Game: Fraction Concentration.
- **Self Assessment:** As students are working through the chapter, encourage them to practise at home. They can use the Skills Bank or Workbook.
- **Journal Writing:** Good opportunities for journal writing occur in the Reflecting or the Consolidation section in any lesson.

Managing Assessment of Learning

- Refer to the last four columns of the Chapter 12 Assessment Chart on the next page. There you will find detailed support for all the Key Assessment Questions in Lessons 1 to 5, and all of the questions in the Mid-Chapter Review and Chapter Review, as well as in the Chapter 12 Task. Which of these opportunities you choose to assess will depend on the quantity of evidence you need to gather for individual students.

    Note: When charts show levels of student achievement, they are always based on the appropriate parts of the four generic rubrics (scoring scales):
  Problem-Solving Rubric (Tool 6)
  Understanding of Concepts Rubric (Tool 7)
  Application of Mathematical Procedures Rubric (Tool 8)
  Communication Rubric (Tool 9)
- If you want to assess other questions from the lessons, the Problem Bank, or the Problems of the Week, use the appropriate rows from the four generic rubrics to create your own question-specific rubric.
- Use any of these instructions and tools to help you record and track student achievement:
  Using the Assessment of Learning Summary—Individual Student
  Assessment of Learning Summary—Individual Student (Tool 10)
  Using the Assessment of Learning Summary—Class by Strand
  Assessment of Learning Summary—Class by Strand (Tool 11)
  Using the Assessment of Learning Skills Chart
  Assessment of Learning Skills Chart (Tool 12)
- **Self Assessment:** After students have completed the chapter, encourage them to try Test Yourself on Workbook page 97. (Answers to these multiple-choice questions and all other Workbook questions can be found at **www.mathk8.nelson.com**.)
- **Journal Writing:** A good opportunity for journal writing occurs in the Chapter Review. Have students reflect on what they have learned about the chapter goals, using a prompt such as, "I can show a fraction by …"

Managing Chapter Evaluation

- Look at the assessment data you've recorded throughout the chapter on Tools 10, 11, and 12. Also include any end-of-chapter information from either the Chapter 12 Task Pages 1 & 2, pp. 50–51 or the Chapter 12 Test Pages 1 & 2, pp. 48–49. Determine the most consistent level for an individual.

Chapter 12 Assessment Chart

Student Book Lesson	Assessment for Feedback Chart	Assessment of Learning			
		Chart	Question/Category	ON Expectations	Strategy
Lesson 1: Guided Activity Fractions as Parts of a Group, pp. 288–289	TR. P. 13	TR. p. 16	5, Understanding of Concepts	3m20	skills demonstration, short answer
Lesson 2: Guided Activity Fractions as Parts of a Whole, pp. 290–291	TR p. 17	TR. p. 20	6, Understanding of Concepts	3m20	short answer
Lesson 3: Guided Activity Communicate Using Drawings, pp. 292–293	TR p. 21	TR p. 24	4, Communication	3m3	written question
Mid-Chapter Review, p. 294		TR pp. 26–27	1, Communication	3m20	written question
			2, Communication	3m20	written question
			3, Understanding of Concepts	3m20	short answer
			4, Understanding of Concepts	3m3	short answer
			5, Communication	3m20	written question
			6, Application of Procedures	3m20	written question
Lesson 4: Exploration Fractions as Parts of a Measure, p. 296	TR p. 29	TR p. 31	entire exploration, Problem Solving	3m8	investigation
Lesson 5: Direct Instruction Mixed Numbers, pp. 298–299	TR p. 33	TR p. 36	6, Communication	3m3	written question
Chapter Review, pp. 304–305		TR pp. 41–42	1, Understanding of Concepts	3m20	short answer
			2, Communication	3m20	written question
			3, Communication	3m3	skills demonstration, written question
			4, Understanding of Concepts	3m20	short answer
			5, Understanding of Concepts	3m20	short answer
			6, Communication	3m3	short answer
			7, Communication	3m8	written question
			8, Understanding of Concepts	3m20	written question
			9, Problem Solving	3m8	skills demonstration
			10, Problem Solving	3m8	written question
Chapter Task, p. 306		TR p. 44	entire task, Understanding of Concepts, Application of Procedures, Communication	3m3, 3m8, 3m20	observation and product making

Reading Strategies

Reading for Understanding	Strategies
Getting Started **Building a mathematical vocabulary:** By understanding the term *fraction*, students will understand the problems that follow.	• Have students explain, in their own words, what a fraction is. • Ask them to check their explanation using the glossary. • Ask them why it is important to study and understand fractions.
Lesson 1 **Using text features to help understand the text:** Students will be able to identify bolded and highlighted words and understand how these words help them read and understand the text.	• Ask students to find words in the text that are written differently than the rest of the text (bolded/highlighted words—numerator, denominator). • Ask students the purpose of these text features. How do these features help them read the text?
Lesson 2 **Reading pictures, numbers, and words:** By reading the pictures, numbers, and words in the example, students will have a better understanding of the concepts.	• Ask students to review Ian's Pizza. • Ask students to describe how Ian solved the problem. • Ask how the use of pictures, numbers, and words in the example helps them understand how to divide the pizza.
Lesson 3 **Communicating mathematically:** By reading Juan's Instructions, students will understand the importance of clear, complete, and organized communications.	• Ask students to explain why it is important to communicate mathematically. • Ask how the drawings helped them understand Juan's instructions. • Ask how Juan could use the Communication Checklist to improve his instructions.
Mid-Chapter Review **Identifying key words and symbols:** By identifying key words in a question, students will better understand how to respond to the question.	• Ask students to identify the words that tell them what they need to do to answer the questions (e.g., describe, model, sketch, show, etc.). • Ask how these key words will help them respond appropriately to the questions.
Math Game **Reading and following procedures to play the Math Game:** By reading through the steps, students will understand how to play Fraction Concentration.	• Ask students to identify what materials they will need to play the game. • Ask how many people can play this game. • Ask them to explain the game in their own words.
Lesson 4 **Reading the problem closely and carefully:** By reading each section of the problem closely and carefully, students will have a clear understanding of what they are being asked to do.	• Ask students to identify the key words in prompts A to E (e.g., fold, fill, explain, show, etc.). • Ask how identifying the key words will help them complete the problem.
Lesson 5 **Reviewing the example:** By carefully reviewing the example, students will have a better understanding of mixed numbers.	• Ask students to explain, in their own words, how Keisha's discovery helped them understand mixed numbers. • Ask how reviewing the example will help them complete the problems that follow.
Skills Bank/Problem Bank/Chapter Review **Finding key information and following directions:** By selecting the key information in a problem and following directions, students will find the information they need to help solve the problems and answer the questions.	• Ask students what they can do to find the key information in the questions in the Skills Bank, and the problems in the Problem Bank and Chapter Review (e.g., read the questions/problems carefully, identify key words, etc.).
Chapter Task **Using the Task Checklist:** By reviewing the Task Checklist, students will have a better understanding of how to complete the task.	• Ask students to explain the purpose of the Task Checklist. • Ask how reviewing the checklist before solving the problem can help them complete the problem.

Chapter Opener

Using the Chapter Opener

Introduce this chapter by discussing the photograph on Student Book page 285, which shows three shelves holding books, wooden toys, and stuffed toys. Note the caption on the photograph, "Favourite collections," and discuss with the students any favourite collections they have. Ask the class questions such as:

- How many shelves are there altogether? (3)
- How many of the shelves hold books? (1)
  How many shelves out of all the shelves hold books? (1 out of 3 or $\frac{1}{3}$)
- How many books are there? wooden toys? stuffed toys? (10 each)
- How many books are lying down on the top shelf? (4)
  How many books are lying down out of all the books? (4 out of 10 or $\frac{4}{10}$)
- How many of the stuffed toys are dolls? (2)
  How many stuffed toys are dolls out of all the toys? (2 out of 10 or $\frac{2}{10}$)
- How many of the stuffed toys are animals? (8)
  How many stuffed toys are animals out of all the toys? (8 out of 10 or $\frac{8}{10}$)

Discuss the title of this chapter, "Fractions," and ask students if they know what the word means. Ask students when they may have seen or used fractions before. Ask them to look through the chapter for examples. Encourage them to pose and answer questions about fractions:

- What fraction of the stuffed toys are monkeys? ($\frac{2}{10}$)
- What fraction of the wooden toys are animals? ($\frac{2}{10}$)
- What fraction of the wooden toys have wheels? ($\frac{10}{10}$)

Be sure to introduce the idea of using a storage closet to organize toys and games, which is the focus of the Chapter Task.

Hold a brief class discussion about the three goals of the chapter. Ask students to record in their journals their thoughts about the first two goals, using a prompt such as: "I can show a fraction by…" At the end of the chapter, you can ask students to complete the same prompt and compare their responses, and reflect on what they have learned. Then ask students if they know what a mixed number is. Explain briefly that a mixed number is a number made up of a whole number and a fraction, and that they will be investigating this further in the chapter.

At this time, it would be appropriate to

- send home the Family Newsletter
- ask students to look through the chapter and add math word cards to your classroom word wall. Here are some terms related to this chapter:

| fraction | numerator | denominator | mixed number |

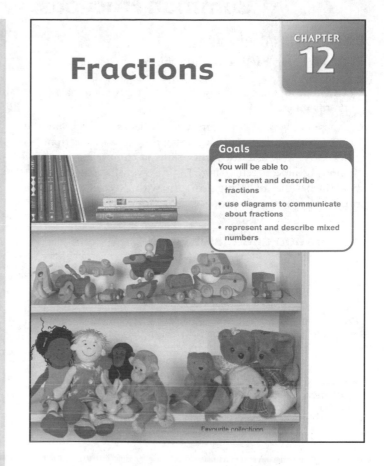

CHAPTER 12

Fractions

Goals

You will be able to

- represent and describe fractions
- use diagrams to communicate about fractions
- represent and describe mixed numbers

Favourite collections

Family Newsletter Master p. 45

Getting Started: Common Fractions

Grade 2 Skills/Concepts

• Compare proper fractions using concrete materials.
• Represent and explain halves, thirds, and quarters as part of a whole and as part of a set using concrete materials and drawings.

Use these pages as an opportunity for initial assessment and to give you a sense of students' understanding of fractions from Grade 2. As well, assess students' skills in comparing proper fractions using concrete materials. Observe what students can do and what they're having difficulty with. Record your notes using the Initial Assessment Summary for each individual.

Preparation and Planning

Pacing	**30–40 min** Activity **10–20 min** Do You Remember?
Materials	• 2-coloured counters, 4/student
Masters	• (for Extra Support) Scaffolding p. 52 • (for Extra Support) Scaffolding p. 53 • Fraction Mats p. 59 • (for Assessment) Initial Assessment Summary, Masters Booklet p. 1
Vocabulary/ Symbols	fraction

Using the Activity (Whole Class) ▶ 30–40 min

Ask students to examine the picture on Student Book page 286, and have them to make a list of the items they see. Begin the list on the board (e.g., 3 pictures on the wall, 1 clock, 4 people, 3 candles, etc.), and then encourage students to continue the list.

Distribute counters and **Fraction Mats p. 59** to students. Take time to compare the fraction mats to the plates on the table. Then guide students through the prompts on Student Book page 287. If Extra Support is required, provide copies of **Scaffolding Master p. 52**.

Prompt A Some students may look at the four plates on the table as a set, and describe it as "$\frac{1}{4}$ of the plates are pie plates." Encourage students to then describe how the eating plates are divided, and ask if each plate has food in the same number of sections.

Prompt B Students may see the three division lines on the glass and say the glass is divided into three parts. Assist them by drawing the glass on the board and colouring each section in a different colour. Students will more readily see the different types of drink in the glasses, and may describe this fraction: $\frac{1}{4}$ of the glasses have orange juice.

Prompt C The people at the table can be described in many ways. Discuss attributes that can be used (e.g., colour of clothing or hair, age, wearing glasses, etc.).

Prompt D At this stage, it is very important that students develop their own definition of a fraction; they should be encouraged to use words, pictures, and numbers in their answer. Have all students share their responses without evaluation. Students may return to these explanations at the end of the chapter and revise what they have written.

Prompt F Students should be encouraged to use words, pictures and numbers in their answer.

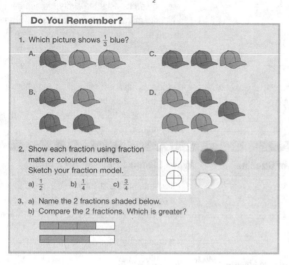

A. What fractions do the plates of food show?

B. What fractions do the drinks show?

C. What fractions describe the people at the table?

D. What is a fraction?

E. Use counters to show $\frac{1}{4}$. Show $\frac{1}{4}$ in a different way.

F. Find examples of the fraction $\frac{1}{2}$ in the picture.

G. Use fraction pieces or counters to show $\frac{1}{2}$ in at least 3 other ways. Explain how each shows $\frac{1}{2}$.

Do You Remember?

1. Which picture shows $\frac{1}{3}$ blue?

2. Show each fraction using fraction mats or coloured counters. Sketch your fraction model.
   a) $\frac{1}{2}$ b) $\frac{1}{4}$ c) $\frac{3}{4}$

3. a) Name the 2 fractions shaded below.
   b) Compare the 2 fractions. Which is greater?

287

Using Do You Remember?
(Individual) ▶ 10–20 min

1. Encourage students to describe each picture in words before determining the fraction. Watch for students who indicate that B represents $\frac{1}{3}$ blue. This shows that they understand that the top number represents blue, but think that the bottom number represents all the rest, instead of the whole. If Extra Support is required, guide those students and provide copies of **Scaffolding Master p. 53**.

2. Using counters, students would show the fractions as parts of a set. Using the fraction mats, they would show fractions as part of a whole. Some students may use the counters on top of the fraction mats, thus showing both representations of a given fraction.

3. Students can visually determine which fraction is greater, but encourage them to use words to describe the fractions. Some students may name the fractions as $\frac{1}{4}$ and $\frac{1}{3}$ instead of $\frac{3}{4}$ and $\frac{2}{3}$. This is not wrong but, throughout the chapter, shading is used to represent the fraction under consideration.

Answers

A. $\frac{1}{3}$, $\frac{2}{3}$

B. $\frac{1}{4}$, $\frac{2}{4}$ (or $\frac{1}{2}$), $\frac{3}{4}$, $\frac{4}{4}$

C. For example, $\frac{3}{4}$ are children, $\frac{1}{4}$ are adults, $\frac{1}{4}$ are wearing glasses, $\frac{4}{4}$ are wearing blue.

D. For example, a fraction is a way of showing the number of equal parts in a whole or in a set.

E. For example:

F. For example, two of the pictures on the wall show $\frac{1}{2}$ blue. The boy's sweater is $\frac{1}{2}$ red and $\frac{1}{2}$ blue. One of the glasses of milk is $\frac{1}{2}$ full.

G. For example:

1. C

2. a) For example:

b) For example:

c) For example:

3. a) $\frac{3}{4}$ and $\frac{2}{3}$

b) $\frac{3}{4}$ is greater than $\frac{2}{3}$.

Common Fractions	When Students Have an Area of Strength	When Students Have an Area of Need
• Prompts A, B, C, & F (Understanding of Concepts)	• Students will identify halves, thirds, and quarters from pictures as a part of a whole and as part of a set.	• Students may more easily recognize unit fractions ($\frac{1}{3}$ or $\frac{1}{4}$, but not $\frac{2}{3}$ or $\frac{3}{4}$), or they may have difficulty recognizing fractions at the pictorial level. Provide students with real objects, such as cutout paper circles, candles, or plates that are divided into sections; students can also act out the scene. Active manipulation of materials will be required.
• Prompts E & G (Understanding of Concepts)	• Students will use counters and drawings to model a unit fraction in three different ways.	• Students who have difficulty modelling a unit fraction can be asked to circle the number that tells how many objects or pieces in all. They should then describe how they will represent the fraction (e.g., I will make $\frac{1}{4}$ of the counters red. There are four counters and one will be red.).
• Prompts D & G (Understanding of Concepts)	• Students will explain the relationships between the model and the fraction it represents, using everyday language.	• If students have difficulty explaining how a model represents a fraction, use the prompt, "The bottom number tells .... There are ___ altogether in my model."

Do You Remember?	When Students Have an Area of Strength	When Students Have an Area of Need
• Question 1 (Understanding of Concepts)	• Students recognize a pictorial representation of $\frac{1}{3}$.	• If students have difficulty, ask them to describe the number of blue hats in each of the diagrams in their own words. Model this by saying, "There are three hats altogether and two are blue." Write the fraction symbols for this as you describe.
• Question 2 (Understanding of Concepts)	• Students can model halves, thirds, and quarters concretely and pictorially.	• Students will often model correctly using the fraction of a whole model (fraction mat) because the division of the whole has been provided, but they may have difficulty modelling with counters. Some students may represent $\frac{1}{4}$ with one red and four blue. To move from one model to the other, have them represent the fraction using the fraction mat, and then place coloured counters on top of each section of the mat.
• Question 3 (Understanding of Concepts)	• Students can compare two fractions using a pictorial model.	• Students who have difficulty naming the fractions should be encouraged to identify the denominator by counting all the pieces, and then finding the number of coloured pieces. Students who have difficulty comparing should create this model, cut out the pieces, and place them on top of each other for comparison

Extra Support:
Scaffolding Master p. 52

Extra Support:
Scaffolding Master p. 53

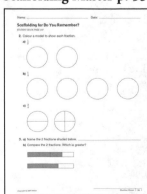

Fraction Mats p. 59

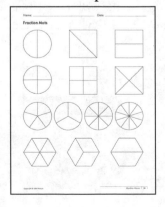

Assessment: Initial
Assessment Summary p. 1

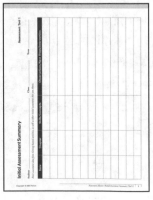

Fractions as Parts of a Group

 Goal Use fractions to describe parts of a group.

Prerequisite Skills/Concepts

- Compare proper fractions using concrete materials.
- Represent and explain halves, thirds, and quarters as part of a set using concrete materials.

Expectations

3m3 represent common fractions [and mixed numbers] using concrete materials

3m20 represent and explain common fractions, presented in real-life situations, as [part of a whole,] part of a set, [and part of a measure] using concrete materials and drawings

Assessment for Feedback	What You Will See Students Doing...	
Students will	**When Students Understand**	**If Students Misunderstand**
• represent common fractions as part of as set	• Students will use a part of a set model (concrete and pictorial) to represent any common fraction.	• Students who have difficulty modelling fractions using a set model should begin by using two-coloured counters. Circle the denominator and place that number of counters on the table. Read the numerator and have the students turn over that number of counters to the second colour. Ask them to describe the set using words.
• explain common fractions presented in real-life situations	• Have students refer to the denominator and numerator to explain their choice of fraction symbol or model for a real-life situation.	• Students may have difficulty explaining more complex fractional representation. Encourage students to always begin with the denominator, which explains how many in the set altogether. Have them support their written explanations by linking to their drawings.

Preparation and Planning

Pacing	**5–10 min** Introduction **15–20 min** Teaching and Learning **20–30 min** Consolidation
Materials	• 2-coloured counters, 10/student • (for Extra Challenge) red and white blocks
Masters	• Mental Math p. 46 • (for Extra Support of Questions 6 & 7) Scaffolding p. 54
Workbook	p. 92
Vocabulary/Symbols	numerator, denominator, fraction
Key Assessment of Learning Question	Question 5, Understanding of Concepts

Meeting Individual Needs

Extra Challenge

- Ask students to show $\frac{1}{3}$ using two different concrete materials of different sizes (for example, one red counter and two white counters, and one red block and two white blocks.) Ask students to explain how the red things are each $\frac{1}{3}$ even though the blocks are larger than the counters. Ask students to describe a set that is $\frac{1}{3}$ red with objects even larger than blocks.
- Challenge students to use coloured counters to show a set that is $\frac{1}{2}$ red, $\frac{1}{3}$ blue, and $\frac{1}{6}$ white.

Extra Support

- Ask students to use counters to show sets that are $\frac{1}{3}$ red, $\frac{2}{3}$ red, $\frac{1}{4}$ red, $\frac{2}{4}$ red, and $\frac{3}{4}$ red.
- Some students may have difficulty using coloured counters to help them represent proper fractions in writing. For example, of two red counters and three white counters, the red counters can be written as $\frac{2}{5}$ and the white counters as $\frac{3}{5}$ of the whole set.

1. Introduction (Whole Class)
▶ 5–10 min

Select four students to come to the front of the room. Make sure one student has an obvious attribute that is different from the other three (for example, one has blonde hair and three have dark hair). Ask students to recall what $\frac{1}{4}$ means (1 out of 4). Ask students to tell you something that is true about $\frac{1}{4}$ of the group (for example, blonde) and something that is true about $\frac{3}{4}$ of the group (for example, dark-haired). Extend the activity by asking students to develop fractions based on other attributes.

Sample Discourse

"What is the same about three of these students, but not the fourth student?"

• *Three have dark hair and one has blonde hair.*

"What fraction of the group has blonde hair?"

• $\frac{1}{4}$

"What fraction of the group has dark hair?"

• $\frac{3}{4}$

"What you say about $\frac{1}{2}$ of the group?"

• $\frac{1}{2}$ *of the group has long hair and the other $\frac{1}{2}$ has short hair.*

Continue with this type of questioning using different groups of four and different attributes. Add another student and continue the activity using fractions that now involve fifths.

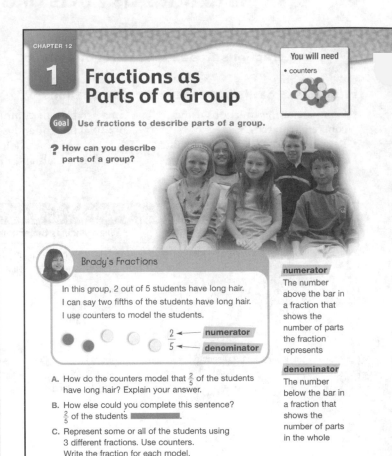

1 Fractions as Parts of a Group

You will need
• counters

Goal Use fractions to describe parts of a group.

? How can you describe parts of a group?

Brady's Fractions

In this group, 2 out of 5 students have long hair. I can say two fifths of the students have long hair. I use counters to model the students.

$\frac{2}{5}$ ← numerator
  ← denominator

A. How do the counters model that $\frac{2}{5}$ of the students have long hair? Explain your answer.

B. How else could you complete this sentence? $\frac{2}{5}$ of the students ▬▬▬▬.

C. Represent some or all of the students using 3 different fractions. Use counters. Write the fraction for each model.

numerator
The number above the bar in a fraction that shows the number of parts the fraction represents

denominator
The number below the bar in a fraction that shows the number of parts in the whole

288   NEL

2. Teaching and Learning (Whole Class/Pairs) ▶ 15–20 min

Have students look at the group photo on Student Book page 288. Ask them to describe the students in the picture. Together, read Brady's description of parts of the group, and ask students to explain if they agree with Brady's response, giving reasons. Ask students to explain what the red counters and what the white counters represent (long hair/not long hair). Make a list of other attributes that might be used to group the students (e.g., colour of clothing, gender, hair decorations, glasses, etc.).

Distribute counters to students, and have them work in pairs to complete prompts A to C. Have the pairs share their answers, encouraging them to find fractions that are different from those modelled by other groups.

Sample Discourse

"How do the counters model that $\frac{2}{5}$ of the students have long hair?"

• *There are five students altogether, so Brady used five counters. Two of the students have long hair, so the two red counters represent the two people with long hair.*

Reflecting

Discuss the questions and encourage different responses.

1. • *The numerator tells me how many students are wearing something blue. The denominator tells me how many students there are altogether. So $\frac{4}{5}$ tells me that four out of five students are wearing blue.*

   • *My fraction is $\frac{1}{3}$. The 1 tells me that one girl has short hair. The 3 tells me that there are three girls.*

2. • *All the students are children. None of the students are adults. So $\frac{5}{5}$ are children and $\frac{0}{5}$ are adults.*

3. • *No, the parts can look different. The two girls with long hair look different.*

   • *The parts do not have to look the same. They just need to have one thing the same. It's the number of parts in the group that's important.*

Reflecting

1. Describe the fractions that you modelled in part C. What does the numerator tell you? What does the denominator tell you?

2. a) What fraction of the students are children?
   b) What fraction are adults?

3. When fractions are used to represent parts of a group, do all the parts have to look the same?

Checking

4. What fraction of each group are children? Explain.

a)    b)

Practising

5. a) Model the fraction $\frac{3}{4}$ using counters and a sketch.
   b) What fraction is *not* red?

6. A kennel has 8 animals. $\frac{3}{8}$ of the animals are cats.
   a) Model the animals with counters and a sketch.
   b) How many animals are not cats?
   c) What fraction are not cats?

7. $\frac{3}{5}$ of a group are girls and $\frac{3}{5}$ have black hair.
   a) Represent the group using counters.
   b) How many children could be in the group?
   c) How many are girls? How many are boys?
   d) How many girls could have black hair?
   e) Suppose a boy with red hair joins the group. Represent the new group with counters and fractions.

— **Key Assessment of Learning question (See chart on next page.)**

NEL   289

Answers

A. For example, there is one counter for each of the five students. The counters for students who have long hair are red. The counters for students who have short hair are white. Two out of the five counters are red, so that shows that $\frac{2}{5}$ of the students have long hair.

B. For example, $\frac{2}{5}$ of the students are boys.

C. For example, $\frac{1}{5}$ of the students is wearing a headband (one red counter and four white counters). $\frac{4}{5}$ of the students are wearing blue clothes (four red counters and one white counter). $\frac{3}{5}$ of the students are girls (three red counters and two white counters).

1. For example, 1 out of 5 students, or $\frac{1}{5}$ of the students, is wearing a headband. The denominator tells me there are five students altogether, and the numerator tells me that one student is wearing a headband.

2. a) $\frac{5}{5}$ **b)** $\frac{0}{5}$

3. For example, no, the parts don't have to be exactly the same. We used fractions to say that $\frac{2}{5}$ of the students have long hair. These two students are different (one has blonde hair, the other dark), but they're both part of the group that has long hair.

3. Consolidation ▶ 20–30 min

Checking (Small Groups)

For intervention strategies, refer to Meeting Individual Needs and the Assessment for Feedback chart.

4. Students should model this question using one colour of counter to represent children and another colour to represent adults.

Practising (Individual)

5. & 6. Both of these questions ask about the fraction that is *not* something. Ensure that students read carefully to see that.

7. There are a number of possible answers to Question 7, depending on how students understand the question. All that is known for sure is that three out of the five are girls and three out of the five have black hair. There may or may not be overlap of those two attributes.

6.–7. If Extra Support is required, provide copies of **Scaffolding Master p. 54**.

Related Questions to Ask

Ask	Possible Response
About **Question 6:** • What other animals might be in the kennel that are not cats? Make up a fraction question about one of the other animals.	• Four of the animals in the kennel are dogs. What fraction are dogs?
About **Question 7:** • Can you say that the three girls in the group have black hair?	• No. All we know is that three people in the group are girls and three people have black hair. The three girls might all have black hair, but maybe only one or two of them have black hair. The other people in the group could have black hair.

Closing (Individual)

To summarize their learning, have student draw a set of 10 people in their journals. Suggest they draw a mix of children and adults, male and female, and noticeable characteristics. Then have them write three different fractions to represent the people in the group; for example, $\frac{2}{10}$ of the people are wearing jeans.

4. a) For example, there are 2 children and 4 people in total, so $\frac{2}{4}$ of the group are children.

b) For example, there are 6 children and 10 people in total, so $\frac{6}{10}$ of the group are children.

(Lesson 1 Answers continued on p. 63)

Assessment Strategy: skills demonstration, short answer
Understanding of Concepts

Question 5

a) Model the fraction $\frac{3}{4}$ using counters and a sketch.

b) What fraction is *not* red?

(Score 1 point for each ✔ for a total of 3.)

Student Name	• correctly models fraction using counters	• correctly sketches model	• correctly states which fraction is not red	Total out of 3
Ryan	✔	✔	✔	3

Extra Practice and Extension

- You might assign any of the questions related to this lesson, which are cross-referenced in the chart below.

Mid-Chapter Review	Student Book p. 294, Questions 1 & 2
Skills Bank	Student Book p. 301, Questions 1 & 2
Problem Bank	Student Book p. 303, Questions 1, 2, & 3
Chapter Review	Student Book p. 304, Questions 1, 2, & 3
Workbook	p. 92, all questions
Nelson Web Site	Visit **www.mathk8.nelson.com** and follow the links to *Nelson Mathematics 3*, Chapter 12.

Math Background

To understand fractions, students must look at the relationships between objects having certain attributes and the whole group of objects. The number of objects is important only as part of the entire set.

The terms *numerator* and *denominator* are important in that they help us to communicate. However, more important is that students understand what the *number on top* and the *number on the bottom* of a fraction represent. The numerator is always the number matching a set criteria or attribute. However, the denominator can represent the total number of objects in a group or it can represent the number of parts that a whole object has been divided into. This latter concept will be dealt with in the next lesson.

At Home

- Students can use playing cards and counters at home to practise modelling fractions as parts of a group with a family member. They choose two cards from a deck at random. Face cards will be worth 10 and all other cards will be their face value. Then they make a fraction by placing the smaller number above the greater number. They can then model the resulting fraction with counters.

Extra Support: Scaffolding Master p. 54

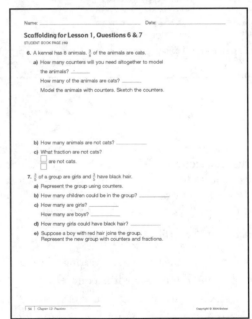

2 Fractions as Parts of a Whole

Goal Use fractions to describe parts of a whole.

Prerequisite Skills/Concepts

- Compare two proper fractions using concrete materials.
- Represent and explain halves, thirds, and quarters as part of a whole using concrete materials.

Expectations

3m3 represent common fractions [and mixed numbers] using concrete materials, drawings, and ordinals

3m20 represent and explain common fractions, presented in real-life situations, as part of a whole, [part of a set, and part of a measure] using concrete materials and drawings

Assessment for Feedback	What You Will See Students Doing...	
Students will	**When Students Understand**	**If Students Misunderstand**
• represent fractions that are parts of a whole using concrete materials and drawings	• Students will model common fractions as parts of a whole using concrete materials and drawings.	• Some students may subdivide the whole into different-sized parts. This may be from poor planning or lack of eye-hand coordination. Provide predivided sections, so that the focus is on determining the number of sections to colour. Grid paper can also be used. • Some students may think that each part must be the same shape. Encourage students to divide the shapes in various ways. For example, each part is $\frac{1}{4}$:
• explain common fractions presented in real-life situations	• Students will use math language, including the terms *numerator* and *denominator*, to describe and explain common fractions in real-life situations.	• Students who have difficulty describing fractional situations in words and symbols should be encouraged to count the fractional parts first to determine the denominator. Post the terms in the classroom, with guiding questions such as, "How many parts are there altogether?" (denominator) and "How many parts are in the group you are describing?" (numerator)

Preparation and Planning

Pacing	**5–10 min** Introduction **15–20 min** Teaching and Learning **20–30 min** Consolidation
Materials	• pencil crayons • pattern blocks
Masters	• Mental Math p. 46 • (for Extra Support of Question 6) Scaffolding p. 55 • Fraction Mats p. 59 • (manipulatives substitute) Pattern Blocks, Masters Booklet pp. 40, 42, 44, 45
Workbook	• p. 93
Key Assessment of Learning Question	Question 6, Understanding of Concepts

Meeting Individual Needs

Extra Challenge

- Students can trace pattern blocks to create designs. They can then colour the designs and write up a description using fractions. (For example, $\frac{2}{10}$ of my design is yellow, $\frac{3}{10}$ is red, and $\frac{5}{10}$ is black.)
- Students can determine how many minutes the fractions $\frac{1}{2}$, $\frac{1}{4}$, and $\frac{3}{4}$ equal.

Extra Support

- Some students may think that the fraction $\frac{1}{2}$ as part of a whole is dependent on the size of the pieces. They may not understand that even though the red trapezoid is much larger than the green triangle, they both represent $\frac{1}{2}$ when the trapezoid is compared to the yellow hexagon and the triangle is compared to the blue rhombus. To encourage understanding, model many concrete examples using the same fraction, but using different sized blocks.

Introduction (Whole Class)
▶ 5–10 min

Distribute a paper circle to each student. Ask students to fold their circles and then open the fold. Have them describe the result using fraction words. Have students fold their circles again, repeating the discussion, and then again, resulting in eight equal pieces of the circle. Ensure that students realize that each piece is one eighth of the circle. Write this in words and symbols on the board and have students print the symbol $\frac{1}{8}$ in each section of their paper circle.

Ask students to describe things that are shaped like their fraction circle.

Tell students that they will be using fraction circles to find out different ways a pizza can be covered with toppings.

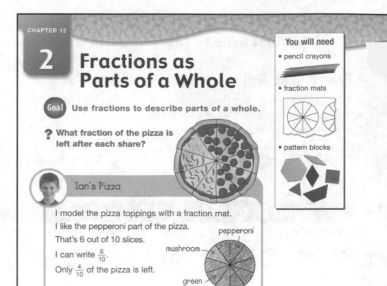

2 Fractions as Parts of a Whole

Goal Use fractions to describe parts of a whole.

? What fraction of the pizza is left after each share?

Ian's Pizza

I model the pizza toppings with a fraction mat.
I like the pepperoni part of the pizza.
That's 6 out of 10 slices.
I can write $\frac{6}{10}$.
Only $\frac{4}{10}$ of the pizza is left.

pepperoni
mushroom
green pepper

You will need
• pencil crayons
• fraction mats
• pattern blocks

A. Brady ate the part of the pizza with green pepper. What fraction of the whole pizza did she eat?

B. What fraction is left after Ian and Brady eat?

C. Lee ate the part of the pizza with mushrooms. What fraction of the whole pizza did he eat?

D. What fraction of the pizza is left after all 3 children eat?

E. What fraction of the pizza did all 3 children eat?

F. Model your own pizza with 8 slices. Cover different slices with different toppings. Use fractions to describe your pizza.

290

NEL

Teaching and Learning (Whole Class/Pairs) ▶ 15–20 min

Draw students' attention to the pizza on Student Book page 290. Ask students to describe any fractions they see. Discuss how the slices are all the same size, which that means that each piece is $\frac{1}{10}$ of the pizza. Read the central question together and work through Ian's Pizza. Focus their attention on the pizza and the model of the pizza.

Provide pairs of students with tenths from **Fraction Mats p. 59**. They may colour the pieces to represent the toppings. Then have them answer prompts A to E and the central question.

Provide pairs with eighths from **Fraction Mats p. 59** and pencil crayons to answer prompt F. Provide time for pairs to share their models and descriptions with the class.

Reflecting

Discuss the questions, encouraging a variety of responses.

Sample Discourse

1. a) • *The pizza had 10 slices, so the denominator would be 10.*

• *The 10 stands for how many pieces the pizza is sliced into. So any fraction about the pizza would have 10 on the bottom.*

b) • *My pizza had a different number of slices.*

• *My pizza is 8 slices, so the denominator in all fractions about my pizza is 8, not 10.*

2. • *If the pizza had 10 slices, 5 is covered with tofu. If it had 8 slices, 4 would be covered with tofu. Both would be $\frac{1}{2}$ of the pizza.*

• *It could have any number of slices as long as $\frac{1}{2}$ of the slices had tofu. It could have 6 slices, and half would be 3. It could have 4 slices, and half would be 2.*

Reflecting

1. a) Why are the denominators for Ian's pizza all the same?
   b) Why is the denominator for your pizza different?

2. Suppose $\frac{1}{2}$ of a pizza is covered with tofu. Do you know how many slices it has? Explain with an example.

Checking

3. Colour a fraction mat so that $\frac{7}{10}$ of a pizza is covered with pineapple.
   a) How many slices does the pizza have?
   b) What do you know about $\frac{3}{10}$ of the pizza?

4. What fraction is coloured?
   a)   b)   c)

Practising

5. Use a different fraction mat for each part. Each time, tell what fraction is covered and what fraction is not.
   a) Cover $\frac{4}{5}$ with tomatoes.
   b) Cover $\frac{2}{3}$ with mushrooms.
   c) Cover $\frac{4}{4}$ with green pepper.

6. Place pattern blocks on the yellow hexagon. What fraction of the hexagon is each shape?
   a) 1 blue rhombus b) 1 red trapezoid c) 1 green triangle

——— Key Assessment of Learning question (See chart on next page.)

NEL 291

---

③ Consolidation ▸ 20–30 min

Checking (Pairs)

For intervention strategies, refer to Meeting Individual Needs or the Assessment for Feedback chart.

3. Provide pairs of students with **Fraction Mats p. 59** and pencil crayons.

4. For each shape, ask if the fraction can be divided or shaded in any other way to represent the same fraction. For example, for part a), you can shade the other half, but you cannot divide this shape any other way to make $\frac{1}{2}$. For part b), you can shade in any three of the five parts in this pentagon, but you cannot divide this shape any other way to make $\frac{1}{5}$. For part c), you can shade in any three of the four parts in this square. There are lots of ways to divide a square into four equal parts and then shade in three to represent $\frac{3}{4}$.

Practising (Individual)

5. Provide **Fraction Mats p. 59** and pencil crayons or counters. Remind students that not all pizzas are round. They may want to use a rectangle as the whole to represent some of the fractions. Students can cut out the mat they want to use and paste it into their notebooks.

6. If Extra Support is required, provide copies of **Scaffolding Master p. 55**.

Related Questions to Ask

Ask	Possible Response
About **Question 5:** • How did you decide how many pieces to divide your pizza into?	• *The denominator told me how many pieces I needed altogether.*
About **Question 6:** • Can you find any other fractions among the pattern blocks?	• *Yes. The green triangle is $\frac{1}{2}$ of the blue rhombus, and it is $\frac{1}{3}$ of the red trapezoid.*

Closing (Individual/Small Group)

Ask students to summarize their learning by writing three or four sentences with fractions that show the concept of parts of a whole. For example, "I was finished colouring $\frac{2}{3}$ of my design when it was time to go home." Have students share and discuss their sentences in small groups.

Answers

A. $\frac{3}{10}$ B. $\frac{1}{10}$ C. $\frac{1}{10}$ D. $\frac{0}{10}$ E. $\frac{10}{10}$

F. For example:

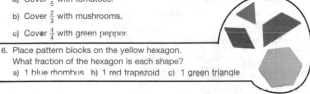

$\frac{4}{8}$ of the pizza has ham.

$\frac{3}{8}$ has pineapple.

$\frac{1}{8}$ has olives.

1. a) For example, the fractions for Ian's pizza are all about different groups of toppings in the same 10-slice pizza, so the denominators are all the same.

   b) For example, the denominator is different because my pizza has been cut into a different number of slices.

2. For example, I don't know how many slices the pizza has. I only know that $\frac{1}{2}$ is covered with tofu. If the pizza were cut into 4 pieces, then 2 of them would be covered with tofu. But if the pizza were cut into 16 pieces, then 8 of them would be covered with tofu.

3. a) 10 b) $\frac{3}{10}$ of the pizza is not covered with pineapple.

4. a) $\frac{1}{2}$ b) $\frac{3}{5}$ c) $\frac{3}{4}$

5. a) For example, $\frac{4}{5}$ is covered with tomatoes and $\frac{1}{5}$ is not.

   b) For example, $\frac{2}{3}$ is covered with mushrooms and $\frac{1}{3}$ is not.

   c) For example, $\frac{4}{4}$ (or the whole pizza) is covered with green peppers.

6. a) $\frac{1}{3}$ b) $\frac{1}{2}$ c) $\frac{1}{6}$

Assessment of Learning—What to Look for in Student Work...

Assessment Strategy: short answer
Understanding of Concepts

Question 6
- Place pattern blocks on the yellow hexagon. What fraction of the hexagon is each shape?
  a) 1 blue rhombus
  b) 1 red trapezoid
  c) 1 green triangle
  (Score correct responses out of 3.)

Extra Practice and Extension

- You might assign any of the questions related to this lesson, which are cross-referenced in the chart below.

Mid-Chapter Review	Student Book p. 294, Questions 3, 4, 5, & 6
Skills Bank	Student Book pp. 301–302, Questions 3, 4, & 5
Problem Bank	Student Book p. 303, Questions 4 & 5
Chapter Review	Student Book pp. 304–305, Questions 4, 5, & 6
Workbook	p. 93, all questions
Nelson Web Site	Visit **www.mathk8.nelson.com** and follow the links to *Nelson Mathematics 3*, Chapter 12.

Math Background

This lesson deals with the concept of fractions as parts of a whole. Wholes can be many shapes and sizes. The important thing to remember is that the denominator tells how many pieces the whole has been divided into equally, and the numerator tells how many pieces have a set criteria, such as being shaded. The greater the number in the denominator, the smaller the pieces that the whole has been divided into.

It is important that students develop the concept of "fair pieces" when determining the number of pieces in a whole. Students need to realize that the pieces should include the same amount, but don't have to be the same shape. Examples and non-examples should be used frequently. For example, non-example of quarters:

At Home

- Encourage students to look for fractions in magazines, newspapers, and books.
- Ask students to find out what toppings each person in their family would like on a pizza slice, and then draw a diagram of the whole pizza. Ask them to explain in words how they shared the pizza.

Extra Support: Scaffolding Master p. 55

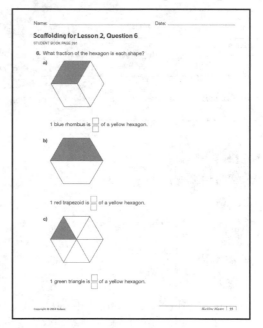

Copyright © 2004 Nelson

3 Communicate Using Drawings

Goal Represent and explain fractions using drawings.

Prerequisite Skills/Concepts
- Recognize halves, thirds, fourths, fifths, sixths, and eighths as parts of wholes.

Expectations
3m3 represent common fractions [and mixed numbers] using concrete materials

3m20 represent and explain common fractions, presented in real-life situations, as part of a whole, [part of a set, and part of a measure] using concrete materials and drawings

Assessment for Feedback	What You Will See Students Doing...	
Students will	**When Students Understand**	**If Students Misunderstand**
• represent fractions that are parts of a whole and parts of a group using drawings	• Students will choose an appropriate model and draw it accurately to represent a fraction.	• Students may have difficulty choosing an appropriate model. Ask students to find concrete models that look like the objects in the Student Book lesson (e.g., a rectangular piece of paper for Question 4). Encourage them to find several different ways to fold the paper to produce the right number of sections.
• explain fractions using drawings	• Students will explain the process used to create a drawing to represent a fraction.	• Some students may have difficulty keeping the instructions in the correct order. Have them work with a partner, with one person folding the paper and the other writing what was done. Once each step is recorded, alter the instructions so that they refer to a drawing.

Preparation and Planning

Pacing	**5–10 min** Introduction **15–20 min** Teaching and Learning **20–30 min** Consolidation
Materials	• scissors, 1 pair/student • (optional) cans • (optional) paper circle, paper rectangle, paper square, 1 each/student
Masters	Mental Math p. 47
Workbook	p. 94
Vocabulary/ Symbols	model, instructions
Key Assessment of Learning Question	Question 4, Communication

Meeting Individual Needs

Extra Challenge
- Students can be challenged to draw one shape and divide it so that they can show $\frac{1}{2}$, $\frac{1}{3}$, $\frac{1}{4}$, and $\frac{1}{6}$ on the shape. (The shape would have to be divided into 12 parts.)
- Have students cut out various shapes from paper, and challenge them to fold each shape into halves, thirds, fourths, fifths, sixths, and eighths. Have them write down on each shape what they could fold it into.

Extra Support
- For students who require extra practice in unit fractions, have them fold circles, rectangles, and squares of paper. After each folding, ask if the parts are equal and how many there are. Ask what fraction would be shown by colouring one of the parts.

1. Introduction (Whole Class)

▶ 5–10 min

Distribute paper to pairs of students, and have them look for ways to fold the paper to make halves and fourths. Have them join with another pair, so each group can teach the other what they have discovered.

Ask students to talk about what parts of their instructions were the most difficult to explain.

Sample Discourse

"What words did you use that helped you explain the directions?"
- *We used words such as diagonal and horizontal.*
- *We used shape words like "make a rectangle when you fold."*

"What can be added to the instructions that would help the person who is following them?"
- *Pictures would help.*
- *A diagram would help us. We could show a picture of each step.*

"Have you ever seen this method used with instructions?"
- *I put a toy together with my Mom. We followed instructions that had both pictures and words.*

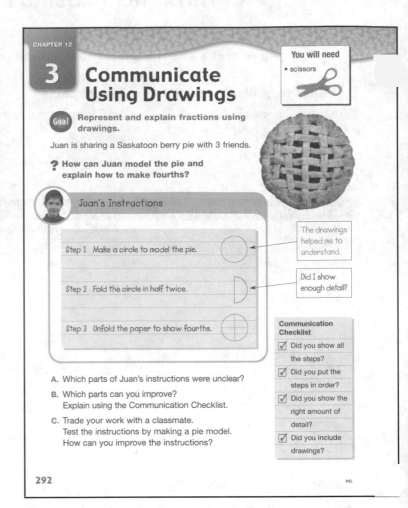

2. Teaching and Learning (Whole Class/Pairs) ▶ 15–20 min

Read the introduction, the central question at the top of Student Book page 292, and Juan's Instructions. Then read the Communication Checklist, ensuring students understand each point. Note the comments on Juan's instructions and how they relate to different steps in the instructions.

Have students work in pairs to answer prompts A to C. Provide each pair with a paper circle or have them trace and cut out their own. Provide cans or other circular objects for tracing.

Sample Discourse

"Let's look at Juan's Instructions. Can you do Step 1?"
- *Yes. I just draw a circle.*

"What does Step 2 tell us to do? What does it show?"
- *Step 2 says to fold the circle in half twice, but the picture shows only that the circle has been folded once. So it only shows halves.*

"How might you change Juan's instructions?"
- *I would say for Step 2 to fold the circle in half once and then show that picture. Then I would say for Step 3 to fold the circle in half again and show that picture. Then Step 4 could say to unfold the paper to show fourths.*

Reflecting

Elicit real life examples from students to talk about why it is important that instructions be in order and be detailed. Ask for examples of when including drawings in instructions would be helpful (in a cookbook, following instructions to make a craft, putting a toy or piece of furniture together, etc.). Talk about what might happen if the instructions weren't in order. Discuss the questions and encourage varied responses.

Sample Discourse

1. a) • *You might not be able to do one instruction until you have done another one before it.*
   b) • *If you leave out a detail, the step might not work the way it should.*
   c) • *Sometimes you can see what to do if you can't read the instructions.*
      • *Drawings can show you exactly what to do. You don't have to guess.*
2. • *If the person can follow the instructions, then you know you did them right.*
   • *You can find out about any parts of the instructions that are not clear.*

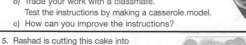
Answers

A. For example, it's not very clear how Juan got from Step 2 to Step 3.

B. For example, I could improve the instructions by adding one more step and giving more detail, like explaining how to make a circle and by using the word "exactly."

Step 1: Trace the bottom of a big can to make a circle and cut it out.

Step 2: Fold the circle exactly in half.

Step 3: Fold the half-circle exactly in half again, but this time from top to bottom.

Step 4: Unfold the circle and trace over the fold lines. Now the circle is divided into fourths. Label the sections from 1 to 4.

C. For example, make the drawings clearer by using dotted lines to show where to fold.

1. a) For example, because you have to know what step comes first, second, etc., to do it right.

   b) For example, if you don't get all the details, you might leave out something important.

Checking (Small Groups)

For intervention strategies, refer to Meeting Individual Needs or the Assessment for Feedback chart.

3. Make sure that students understand that Juan is sharing with seven friends and that he is included, so that the pie needs to be divided into eighths. Have students share their instructions in the group before answering parts b) and c).

Practising (Individual)

4. & 5. Even though both of the questions deal with sixths, the size and shape of $\frac{1}{6}$ in each question is quite different. Reinforce the idea that the important thing is that all the sixths in the casserole are the same size, and all the sixths in the cake are all the same size.

Provide students with a rectangular paper shape, or have them make and cut one out for their model.

Related Questions to Ask

Ask	Possible Response
About **Question 4:** • Would the instruction, "Make a diagonal cut from one corner of the pan to the other," be a good first instruction for cutting the casserole into sixths?	• No, because you would get two triangles, and then each of them would have to be cut into thirds. It would be very hard to get three equal pieces.
About **Question 5:** • How can you cut the cake so that the pieces are quadrilaterals instead of triangles?	• Use three cuts, but instead of cutting from corner to corner, cut from the middle of one side to the middle of the opposite side.

Closing (Pairs)

Have students work in pairs to give their partners instructions for dividing a shape into fractions. One partner can explain how to divide a rectangle into eighths, while the other models each step. Then they can switch roles and the other partner can explain how to divide a circle into eighths, while the first partner models each step.

c) For example, drawings are sometimes easier to follow than written instructions.

2. For example, because different people understand things in different ways. Something that is clear to you might not be clear to your partner.

(Lesson 3 Answers continued on p. 63)

Assessment Strategy: written question
Communication

Question 4
- Sharleen needs to cut a potato casserole for a family of 6.
  a) Write instructions for modelling a casserole cut in sixths.
  b) Trade your work with a classmate. Test the instructions by making a casserole model.
  c) How can you improve the instructions?

1	2	3	4
• provides incomplete or inaccurate instructions that lack clarity or logical thought	• provides partial instructions that exhibit some clarity	• provides complete, clear, and logical instructions for modelling a casserole cut in sixths	• provides thorough, clear, and insightful instructions for modelling a casserole cut in sixths
• organization of written instructions is minimal and seriously impedes communication	• organization of written instructions is limited but does not seriously impede communication	• organization of written instructions is sufficient to support communication	• organization of written instructions is effective and aids communication
• uses drawings that exhibit minimal clarity and accuracy, and are ineffective in communicating	• uses drawings that lack clarity and accuracy, though not sufficient to impede communication	• uses drawings that are sufficiently clear and accurate to communicate	• uses drawings that are clear, precise, and effective in communicating
• uses very little mathematical language correctly	• uses some mathematical language correctly	• uses mathematical language correctly	• uses precise mathematical language

Extra Practice and Extension

- You might assign any of the questions related to this lesson, which are cross-referenced in the chart below.

Chapter Review	Student Book p. 305, Question 7
Workbook	p. 94, all questions
Nelson Web Site	Visit **www.mathk8.nelson.com** and follow the links to *Nelson Mathematics 3*, Chapter 12.

At Home

- Students can practise simple origami folding at home. Suggest that students explain the instructions to a family member while they do each step.
- Have students explain to family members how they would cut or divide appropriate food (such as pizza, square or rectangular casseroles, or cakes) into sixths, eighths, or tenths.

Math Background

In this lesson, students use drawings to help communicate instructions for dividing shapes into fractions. The actual folding of models will be easier for most than drawing the models and writing the instructions. It is important that students use models at this stage to help develop their visualization skills. Communicating with drawings will also help to develop visualization.

Mid-Chapter Review

Using the Mid-Chapter Review

Use this page to assess students' understanding of the concepts developed in the chapter so far. Refer to the assessment chart on pages 26–27 for the details of each question.

Materials: 2-coloured counters

1. Students can use coloured counters to model the answer before sketching.

6. Ensure that students understand that they are to sketch one group of shapes for which all the statements are true.

Related Questions to Ask

Ask	Possible Response
About **Question 2:** • Can you make up another fraction question about these hats?	• What fraction of the hats have a ribbon?
About **Question 6:** • How do you know how many shapes are in the group?	• The clues are about fractions that have a denominator of 5, so I know that I need five shapes so I could figure out the fifths.
• What shapes are in the group?	• I know from the clues that three of the five shapes are rectangles and one shape is a circle. So I can make the last shape whatever I want.

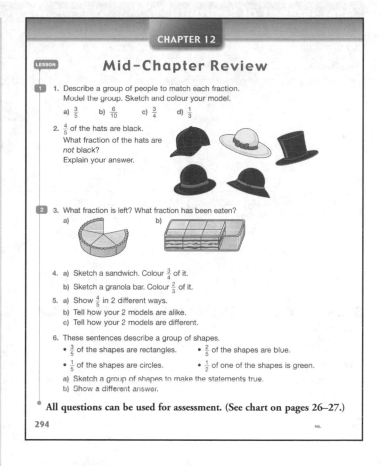

CHAPTER 12

Mid-Chapter Review

1. Describe a group of people to match each fraction. Model the group. Sketch and colour your model.
   a) $\frac{3}{5}$ b) $\frac{6}{10}$ c) $\frac{3}{4}$ d) $\frac{1}{3}$

2. $\frac{4}{5}$ of the hats are black. What fraction of the hats are *not* black? Explain your answer.

3. What fraction is left? What fraction has been eaten?
   a)   b)

4. a) Sketch a sandwich. Colour $\frac{3}{4}$ of it.
   b) Sketch a granola bar. Colour $\frac{2}{3}$ of it.

5. a) Show $\frac{4}{5}$ in 2 different ways.
   b) Tell how your 2 models are alike.
   c) Tell how your 2 models are different.

6. These sentences describe a group of shapes.
   • $\frac{3}{5}$ of the shapes are rectangles.   • $\frac{2}{5}$ of the shapes are blue.
   • $\frac{1}{5}$ of the shapes are circles.   • $\frac{1}{2}$ of one of the shapes is green.
   a) Sketch a group of shapes to make the statements true.
   b) Show a different answer.

All questions can be used for assessment. (See chart on pages 26–27.)

294

Answers

1. a) For example, in a group of 5, there are 3 wearing glasses and 2 not wearing glasses.

   b) For example, in a group of girls, 6 have long hair and 4 have short hair.

   c) For example, in a group of boys, 3 have red shirts and 1 has a blue shirt.

   d) For example, in a group of 3 women, 1 is wearing a hat and the other 2 aren't.

2. $\frac{1}{5}$. There are 5 hats and 4 are black, so 1 out of the 5 is not black. 1 out of 5 is $\frac{1}{5}$.

3. a) $\frac{4}{5}$ is left; $\frac{1}{5}$ has been eaten

   b) $\frac{5}{8}$ is left; $\frac{3}{8}$ has been eaten

4. a) For example:

   b) For example:

5. a) For example:

   b) For example, both of my models show fifths, with four parts coloured.

   c) For example, the circles show parts of a set and the rectangle shows parts of a whole.

6. a) For example:

   b) For example:

Assessment of Learning—What to Look for in Student Work...

Assessment Strategy: written question
Communication

Question 1

- Describe a group of people to match each fraction. Model the group. Sketch and colour your model.

  a) $\frac{3}{5}$

  b) $\frac{6}{10}$

  c) $\frac{3}{4}$

  d) $\frac{1}{3}$

1	2	3	4
• provides incomplete or inaccurate descriptions that lack clarity or logical thought	• provides partial descriptions that exhibit some clarity	• provides complete, clear, and logical descriptions of groups of people to match each fraction	• provides thorough, clear, and insightful descriptions of groups of people to match each fraction
• uses models and coloured sketches that exhibit minimal clarity and accuracy, and are ineffective in communicating	• uses models and coloured sketches that lack clarity and accuracy, though not sufficient to impede communication	• uses models and coloured sketches that are sufficiently clear and accurate to communicate	• uses models and coloured sketches that are clear, precise, and effective in communicating

Assessment Strategy: written question
Communication

Question 2

- $\frac{4}{5}$ of the hats are black. What fraction of the hats are *not* black? Explain your answer.

1	2	3	4
• provides incomplete or inaccurate explanation that lacks clarity or logical thought	• provides partial explanation that exhibits some clarity	• provides complete, clear, and logical explanation for the answer	• provides thorough, clear, and insightful explanation for the answer

Assessment Strategy: short answer
Understanding of Concepts

Question 3

- What fraction is left? What fraction has been eaten?
  (Score 1 point for each correct response for a total out of 4.)

Assessment Strategy: written question
Understanding of Concepts

Question 4

a) Sketch a sandwich. Colour $\frac{3}{4}$ of it.

b) Sketch a granola bar. Colour $\frac{2}{3}$ of it.

(Score correct responses out of 2.)

Assessment Strategy: written question
Communication

Question 5

a) Show $\frac{4}{5}$ in 2 different ways.

b) Tell how your 2 models are alike.

c) Tell how your 2 models are different.

1	2	3	4
• uses models of $\frac{4}{5}$ that exhibit minimal clarity and accuracy, and are ineffective in communicating • provides incomplete or inaccurate explanations that lack clarity or logical thought and use very little mathematical language	• uses models of $\frac{4}{5}$ that lack clarity and accuracy, though not sufficient to impede communication • provides partial explanations that exhibit some clarity and use some mathematical language	• uses models of $\frac{4}{5}$ that are sufficiently clear and accurate to communicate • provides complete, clear, and logical explanations of how the two models are alike and how they are different, using appropriate mathematical language	• uses models of $\frac{4}{5}$ that are clear, precise and effective in communicating • provides thorough, clear, and insightful explanations of how the two models are alike and how they are different, using precise mathematical language

Assessment Strategy: written question
Application of Procedures

Question 6

• These sentences describe a group of shapes.

  • $\frac{3}{5}$ of the shapes are rectangles.

  • $\frac{1}{5}$ of the shapes are circles.

  • $\frac{2}{5}$ of the shapes are blue.

  • $\frac{1}{2}$ of one of the shapes is green.

a) Sketch a group of shapes to make the statements true.

b) Show a different answer.

1	2	3	4
• makes major errors and/or omissions when sketching two different groups of shapes that make the statements true	• makes several errors and/or omissions when sketching two different groups of shapes that make the statements true	• makes only a few errors and/or omissions when sketching two different groups of shapes that make the statements true	• makes almost no errors when sketching two different groups of shapes that make the statements true

Math Game: Fraction Concentration

Using the Math Game

Materials: scissors

Masters: Fraction Concentration Cards pp. 57–58

The master has 12 cards with fractions and 12 matching models of the fractions. You may want to make more cards with other fractions to make the game more challenging.

Object of the Game

From an array of cards turned upside-down, students take turns flipping over two cards at a time. If a player chooses and recognizes a fraction and its matching model, the player keeps both cards and takes another turn. If the cards don't match, the cards are turned back upside-down and the other player chooses. Play continues until all the cards are gone. The player with the most cards wins.

When to Play

Students can play this game after they have a good understanding of fractions as part of a set. Students must also recognize and understand the written form of a proper fraction.

Strategies

At the start of this game, some luck is involved in making matches. However, as the game progresses and more cards are turned over, players may remember where certain cards are placed. Individuals may use certain strategies for memorizing where specific cards are. Ask students to share their memorization strategies.

To make matches, students must recognize the pictorial models for the written proper fractions and vice versa.

Observe

Watch for students who are unable to correctly match fractions with their models. Also, look for students who do not appear to employ a strategy to memorize where certain cards are.

Discuss

As they play, ask students questions such as:

- How do you know that that model represents that fraction?
- How do you know that that fraction represents that model?
- Do you have a way of remembering where certain cards are?

Variations

- Rather than laying the fraction cards out in an array, the cards can just be scattered upside-down on a desktop. This will make it more difficult for students to memorize where certain cards are.
- For a much simpler, more cooperative game, place the cards in an array face up. One player chooses a fraction card or a model card, and the other player must find its match within a specific time.

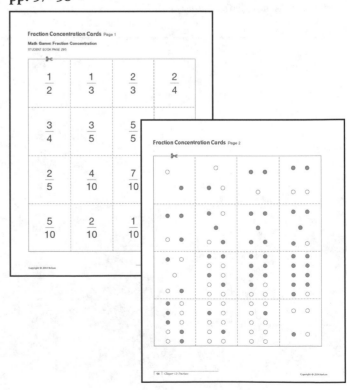

Fraction Concentration Cards pp. 57–58

4 Fractions as Parts of a Measure

Goal Use fractions to describe parts of a measure.

Prerequisite Skills/Concepts

- Compare proper fractions using concrete materials.

Expectations

3m3 represent common fractions [and mixed numbers] using concrete materials

3m8 solve problems and describe and explain the variety of strategies used

3m20 represent and explain common fractions, presented in real-life situations, as [part of a whole, part of a set, and] part of a measure using concrete materials [and drawings]

Assessment for Feedback	What You Will See Students Doing...	
Students will	**When Students Understand**	**If Students Misunderstand**
• represent common fractions as parts of a measure	• Students will create and draw a measurement model to represent common fractions.	• Students who have difficulty folding the ribbon should count the number of pieces they have after each fold. They can use a drawing to record as they move through the steps. Ask, "If I fold the halves in half again, how many pieces will I get?"
• explain common fractions, presented in real-life situations as parts of a measure	• Students will explain how a fraction can be represented using various measurement models.	• Students who have difficulty with volume or time models should be asked to cover the glass or the clock with coloured paper (e.g., a strip on the side of the glass that they have folded into fourths, or a circle that has been folded into fourths).
		• Some students may have difficulty explaining their procedures. Pair these students with others who can assist with the recording. Remind students to use the Communication Checklist from Lesson 3.

Preparation and Planning

Pacing	**5–10 min** Introduction **25–35 min** Teaching and Learning **10–15 min** Consolidation
Materials	• ribbon or strip of paper, 1 piece/student • glass and water, 1/group • a clock with movable hands, 1/group • (optional) calendar, a ruler, a metre stick, various sizes of containers
Masters	• Mental Math p. 47 • (for Assessment) Problem Solving Rubric, Masters Booklet p. 7
Workbook	p. 95
Vocabulary/Symbols	capacity
Key Assessment of Learning Question	Entire Exploration, Problem Solving

Meeting Individual Needs

Extra Challenge

- Students can investigate all of the fractions that they can using a clock and determining the minutes (for example, $\frac{2}{3}$ hour = ■ minutes).
- Students can develop statements with fractions related to years, months, and days (for example, 1 day is $\frac{1}{7}$ of a week; 2 weeks is about $\frac{2}{4}$ of a month).

Extra Support

- To help with fractions of time, start with one hour as the whole. Ask the student to put both hands of the clock on 12. Ask, "How would you show one hour by moving the minute hand?" Remind students that the clock face is a circle. Ask, "How would you show $\frac{1}{2}$ of an hour using the minute hand? Where does the minute hand stop? How would you show $\frac{1}{4}$ of an hour? Where does the minute hand stop?"
- Have students estimate capacity fractions by asking them to fill a glass $\frac{1}{2}$ full of water. Try other fractions such as $\frac{1}{3}$, $\frac{2}{3}$ and $\frac{3}{4}$.

1. Introduction (Whole Class)
▶ 5–10 min

Ask where students have heard or seen people using fractions in measurements. (People use fractions in cooking a lot. Sometimes people only want part of something, like $\frac{1}{2}$ a piece of pie, or $\frac{1}{3}$ a glass of juice.)

2. Teaching and Learning
(Small Groups) ▶ 25–35 min

Draw students' attention to the central question on Student Book page 296. Arrange them in small groups to explore prompts A to E. For prompts A and B, provide a piece of ribbon or a strip of paper for each student. For prompt C, provide glasses that are close to cylindrical in shape.

For prompt E, you can have available a table full of measurement items to stimulate thought. Some items might be a calendar, a ruler, a metre stick, and various sizes of containers (to be filled).

Sample Discourse

"How can you find the $\frac{1}{2}$ point of this ribbon?"
- *You can fold the ribbon so the edges meet.*

"How can you find $\frac{1}{4}$ of a ribbon?"
- *When we folded the ribbon the first time, it was like dividing the ribbon into two parts so each part is $\frac{1}{2}$. If we fold it again, it is like dividing the whole ribbon into four parts, so each part is $\frac{1}{4}$.*

"How do you know that the glass is half full of water?"
- *I just kept pouring until it looked $\frac{1}{2}$ full.*
- *I used the ribbon to measure how tall the glass was and then just folded the ribbon in $\frac{1}{2}$. Then I filled the glass to the height of the fold.*
- *I used a ruler to measure how tall the glass was. Then I filled the glass until the water came to $\frac{1}{2}$ of the height of the glass.*

"What other fractions can you think of that have to do with time? Can you make up a fraction that has to do with weeks and months?"
- *February has 4 weeks, so 1 week would be $\frac{1}{4}$ of the month.*
- *A whole year has 12 months, so 1 month would be $\frac{1}{12}$ of the year.*

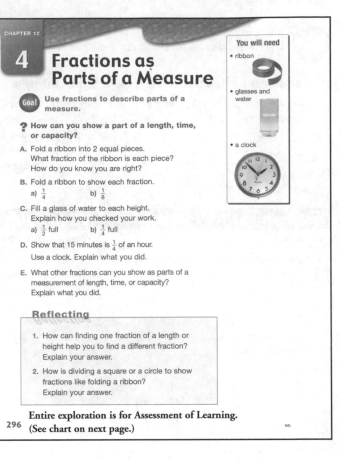

CHAPTER 12

4 Fractions as Parts of a Measure

Goal Use fractions to describe parts of a measure.

? How can you show a part of a length, time, or capacity?

A. Fold a ribbon into 2 equal pieces. What fraction of the ribbon is each piece? How do you know you are right?

B. Fold a ribbon to show each fraction.
 a) $\frac{1}{4}$ b) $\frac{1}{8}$

C. Fill a glass of water to each height. Explain how you checked your work.
 a) $\frac{1}{2}$ full b) $\frac{1}{4}$ full

D. Show that 15 minutes is $\frac{1}{4}$ of an hour. Use a clock. Explain what you did.

E. What other fractions can you show as parts of a measurement of length, time, or capacity? Explain what you did.

You will need
- ribbon
- glasses and water
- a clock

Reflecting

1. How can finding one fraction of a length or height help you to find a different fraction? Explain your answer.

2. How is dividing a square or a circle to show fractions like folding a ribbon? Explain your answer.

Entire exploration is for Assessment of Learning. (See chart on next page.)

296   NEL

Reflecting

Encourage students to think about what they did in the explanation to help them with the Reflecting questions. Discuss the questions, encouraging a variety of responses.

Sample Discourse

1. • *I know that if I divide a length into a number of equal parts, such as 4 parts, that each part is $\frac{1}{4}$. If I divide each of those 4 parts in $\frac{1}{2}$, I get 8 parts and each part is $\frac{1}{8}$. So having $\frac{1}{4}$ can help me find $\frac{1}{8}$ of something.*
   • *If I have $\frac{1}{2}$ a glass of water, I can divide that into 2 parts to find out how much $\frac{1}{4}$ glass of water is.*

2. • *I think of the square or circle as the whole thing. I think of the length of ribbon as the whole thing. Then when I divide or fold, I get parts of the whole.*
   • *Dividing up the whole of anything is the same. The way you divide is different, but you end up with equal parts of the whole thing.*

3. Consolidation ▶ 10–15 min

For intervention strategies, refer to Meeting Individual Needs or the Assessment for Feedback chart.

Closing (Pairs)

Have students work with a partner to estimate where $\frac{1}{2}$, $\frac{1}{4}$, and $\frac{3}{4}$ would be if they were measuring from their shoulders to their fingertips. Then have them check their estimations with a ribbon. Have them do the same activity using the lengths from their hips to the bottom of their feet.

Answers

☞ **A.** $\frac{1}{2}$; for example, because there are two equal pieces and each one is 1 out of 2.

☞ **B. a)** For example:

☞ **b)** For example:

☞ **C. a)** For example, measure straight up the side of the glass with a ribbon, and cut the ribbon so that it's as long as the side. Fold the ribbon into two equal pieces. Hold the folded ribbon, showing $\frac{1}{2}$ the height of the glass, beside the glass and fill up to where the ribbon reaches.

b) For example, fold the ribbon from part a) into two equal pieces. Hold the folded ribbon, showing $\frac{1}{4}$ the height of the glass, beside the glass and fill up to where the ribbon reaches.

☞ **D.** For example, divide the clock face into fourths by dividing it in half across and up and down. The area covered by the minute hand on the clock face in 15 minutes is the same as $\frac{1}{4}$ of a circle.

☞ **E.** For example, I can find $\frac{1}{2}$ of a metre stick because I know that a metre stick has 100 cm, and half that is 50 cm. So half the metre stick would be at the 50 cm mark. I can find $\frac{1}{3}$ of a piece of ribbon by folding it into three equal pieces. Then I can fold it again to get six equal pieces or $\frac{1}{6}$.

☞ **1.** For example, if you have $\frac{1}{2}$, you can get $\frac{1}{4}$ by halving the half. That way you get four equal parts.

☞ **2.** For example, you can think of folding the square in half to make two pieces, just like you folded the ribbon. Or you can fold it into other parts, just like you folded the ribbon.

Assessment of Learning—What to Look for in Student Work...

Assessment Strategy: investigation
The focus is on Problem Solving.

Assessment Opportunity
In this lesson, the entire exploration is an opportunity for assessment. You will see students carrying out an inquiry and will be able to observe their ability to use concrete materials (i.e., ribbons, glasses of water, and clocks) to demonstrate and explain how fractions can be used to describe parts of a measure.

To gather evidence about a student's ability to problem solve, use informal observation, questioning, and written work. Use Problem-Solving Rubric (Tool 6), Masters Booklet, p. 7, to help you focus on the problem-solving process. You may want to focus on the Carry Out the Plan, Look Back, and Communicate rows in the rubric.

Extra Practice and Extension

- You might assign any of the questions related to this lesson, which are cross-referenced in the chart below.

Skills Bank	Student Book p. 302, Questions 6 & 7
Problem Bank	Student Book p. 303, Question 6
Chapter Review	Student Book p. 305, Questions 8 & 9
Workbook	p. 95, all questions
Nelson Web Site	Visit **www.mathk8.nelson.com** and follow the links to *Nelson Mathematics 3*, Chapter 12.

At Home

- Students can bake with family members and talk about the ingredient amounts that involve fractions.
- Students can work with family members to plan trips using a map, and estimate then measure to find a spot $\frac{1}{4}$, $\frac{1}{2}$, etc. along the route.

Math Background

Measurement is continuous—the units are all joined together. When we take a fraction as part of a measure, it is the same as taking a fraction as part of a whole. Even though finding the $\frac{1}{2}$ point on a length of wall is physically quite different than finding the $\frac{1}{2}$ point on a glass, or finding the halfway point in a year, the concept is the same. The thing being measured is considered the whole and the parts of the whole are the fractions of measure.

Curious Math: Fraction Neighbours

Using Curious Math

Students can explore and discover for themselves the patterns and relationships among simple fractions. While doing so, students will encounter the important concept that given unit fractions, the larger the denominator (the number of parts), the smaller each part.

Related Questions to Ask

Ask	Possible Response
About **Questions 1–5:** • How can you explain to someone that if the numerator is always 1, the larger the denominator gets the smaller the fraction is?	• *The denominator tells how many parts a whole is divided into. The more parts there are in a whole, the smaller the part has to be.*

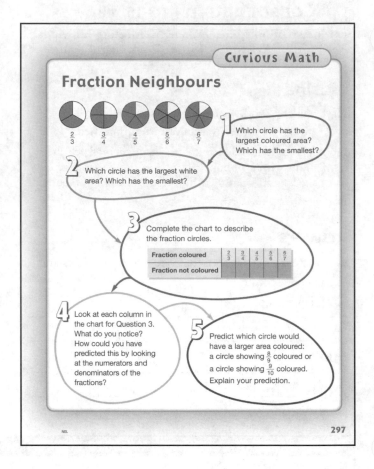

Answers

1. The $\frac{6}{7}$ circle has the largest coloured area, and the $\frac{2}{3}$ circle has the least.

2. The $\frac{2}{3}$ circle has the largest white area, and the $\frac{6}{7}$ circle has the smallest.

3.

Fraction coloured	$\frac{2}{3}$	$\frac{3}{4}$	$\frac{4}{5}$	$\frac{5}{6}$	$\frac{6}{7}$
Fraction not coloured	$\frac{1}{3}$	$\frac{1}{4}$	$\frac{1}{5}$	$\frac{1}{6}$	$\frac{1}{7}$

4. For example, the numerator of every fraction in the bottom row is 1. I could have predicted this because in each circle only one part is not coloured.

5. A circle showing $\frac{9}{10}$ coloured would have more area coloured than a circle showing $\frac{8}{9}$ coloured. I predict this because 10 parts are more than 9 parts, so a part that is $\frac{1}{10}$ will be smaller than a part that is $\frac{1}{9}$.

5 Mixed Numbers

Goal Model and describe mixed numbers.

Prerequisite Skills/Concepts

- Compare proper fractions using concrete materials.
- Represent and explain halves, thirds, fourths, and sixths using concrete materials and drawings.

Expectations

3m3 represent [common fractions and] mixed numbers using concrete materials, drawings, and ordinals

Assessment for Feedback	What You Will See Students Doing...	
Students will	**When Students Understand**	**If Students Misunderstand**
• represent mixed numbers using concrete materials	• Students will use parts of a whole model to represent a mixed number, using a variety of concrete materials.	• Students who have difficulty should create each model using pattern blocks. Once they have decided which pattern block represents one whole, discuss what has been added to the whole. Use everyday language to describe the situation (e.g., "I see one hexagon and $\frac{4}{6}$ of a hexagon."), and de-emphasize the focus on the symbolic.

Preparation and Planning

Pacing	**5 10 min** Introduction **15–20 min** Teaching and Learning **20–30 min** Consolidation
Materials	• pattern blocks: hexagon, trapezoid, rhombus, triangle • (for Extra Support) paper squares
Masters	• Mental Math p. 47 • (for Extra Support of Questions 6, 7, & 8) Scaffolding p. 56 • (manipulatives substitute) Pattern Blocks, Masters Booklet pp. 40, 42, 44, 45
Workbook	p. 96
Vocabulary/ Symbols	mixed number
Key Assessment of Learning Question	Question 6, Communication

Meeting Individual Needs

Extra Challenge

- Students can create word problems such that the answer is a mixed number. For example, Mona had enough muffin batter to make 18 muffins. Each muffin tray held 12 muffins. How many trays could Mona fill? They can exchange problems with classmates to solve.

Extra Support

- Provide students with paper squares. Ask them to use the squares to show you mixed numbers such as $1\frac{1}{4}$, $2\frac{1}{2}$, $3\frac{1}{4}$, etc. They can either fold or colour the square that will represent the fraction parts of the numbers.

Introduction (Whole Class)
▶ 5–10 min

Distribute scrap paper to students. Ask them to hold up one piece of paper, and then two pieces of paper. Then ask students to hold up two and one-half pieces of paper. Have students describe what they did to create two and one-half pieces of paper.

Sample Discourse

"Is two and one-half pieces of paper smaller or larger than two pieces of paper?"
• *It is larger because I have two pieces and then some more.*

"Is it smaller or larger than three pieces of paper? How do you know?"
• *It is smaller. I need another half to make three pieces of paper.*
• *It is smaller because I only have two pieces and then a bit more.*

Have students think of other examples where we might use a whole number and a fraction to describe something. Make a list on the board. (For example, I walk $5\frac{1}{2}$ blocks to school. It takes $1\frac{1}{4}$ hours play the game.)

Tell students that these numbers are called mixed numbers and that today they will learn more about them.

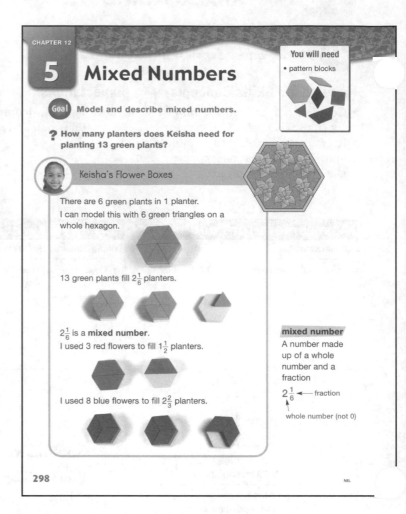

Teaching and Learning (Whole Class/Pairs) ▶ 15–20 min

Have students look at the flower box at the top of Student Book page 298. Ask how many green plants fit into one flower box. In pairs, have students model this by using the yellow hexagon to represent the flower box and the green triangles to represent the green plants. Then have them read the central question and use blocks to find out how many flower boxes Keisha needs for 13 green plants.

Have students model the other examples with the blocks. They should use the yellow hexagon and red trapezoid blocks for the second example, and the yellow hexagon and blue rhombus blocks for the third example.

Sample Discourse

"Keisha has 13 green plants. How many flower boxes can she fill completely? How many plants does she have left?"
• *Two flower boxes. She has one green plant left.*

"Why is that one green plant equal to $\frac{1}{6}$?"
• *There is only one green plant left to plant, but six places in the flower box. So filling in one place out of six is $\frac{1}{6}$.*

Ask similar questions as students model the red and blue flowers.

Reflecting

Discuss the questions, encouraging a variety of responses.

Sample Discourse

1. • *The 2 in the mixed number $2\frac{1}{2}$ is a whole number, and it tells that two whole planters are filled.*
   • *There are two whole planters filled and $\frac{1}{2}$ of a third one.*

2. • *A mixed number has a whole number and a fraction. $1\frac{3}{4}$ has a whole number and a fraction. $\frac{3}{4}$ does not have a whole number.*
   • *$\frac{3}{4}$ is less than a whole, so it can't be a mixed number.*

"How would you write that as a fraction? How would you write that as a whole number?"
• *You could write it as $\frac{4}{4}$, or as 1 whole.*

Reflecting

1. How many whole planters are filled when $2\frac{1}{2}$ planters are planted?

2. Why do we call $1\frac{3}{4}$ a mixed number, but not $\frac{3}{4}$?

Checking

3. Write a mixed number for each model.

    a)   b)

4. More than 2 but less than 3 flower boxes are planted. Model 3 mixed numbers that might represent the flower boxes. Write the mixed numbers.

Practising

5. Write a mixed number for each model.

    a)   b)

6. Model each mixed number. Sketch each model.
    a) $2\frac{2}{3}$ b) $3\frac{1}{6}$

7. Ian took 4 sandwiches for lunch. He ate 1 whole sandwich and $\frac{1}{2}$ of another. He gave the rest to his friends. Sketch pictures to show what Ian ate and what he gave away. Write the mixed numbers.

8. Which model represents $2\frac{3}{4}$? How do you know?

    A.   B.

— **Key Assessment of Learning question (See chart on next page.)**

NEL   299

---

3. Consolidation ♦ 20–30 min

Checking (Pairs)

For intervention strategies, refer to Meeting Individual Needs or the Assessment for Feedback chart.

3. The two parts of this question each use different shapes to model the whole. Discuss with students why this is possible.

Practising (Individual)

7. Even though this can be viewed as a subtraction question $(4 - 1\frac{1}{2})$, the intent of this question is not computation with fractions. Rather, the intent is to see how students will model the sandwiches to see $1\frac{1}{2}$ sandwiches in a set of 4. The other part of the set represents what Ian gave away.

6.–8. If Extra Support is required, provide students with copies of **Scaffolding Master p. 56**.

Related Questions to Ask

Ask	Possible Response
About **Question 6:** • Can you model each mixed number in another way?	• Yes. I used squares to represent the whole numbers, but I could use circles or another shape.
About **Question 8 b):** • What would be the fraction name for each of the whole squares in this question?	• $\frac{4}{4}$

Closing (Individual/Small Groups)

Put the following four mixed numbers on the board: $4\frac{1}{2}$, $2\frac{3}{4}$, $1\frac{1}{4}$, $3\frac{1}{2}$. Ask students to write four clues or questions in their journals that would have as an answer each of the mixed numbers. (For example, "I ate 4 cookies and $\frac{1}{2}$ of another cookie. How many cookies did I eat?") Students can share their clues/questions in groups and answer them.

Answers

1. 2

2. $1\frac{3}{4}$ is a mixed number because it has a whole number part and a fraction part. $\frac{3}{4}$ is a fraction because it only has a fraction part.

3. a) $1\frac{4}{6}$ b) $1\frac{3}{4}$

4. For example:

    $2\frac{1}{2}$

    $2\frac{1}{4}$

    $2\frac{1}{3}$

5. a) $3\frac{1}{6}$ b) $3\frac{2}{3}$

6. a) For example:

    b) For example:

7. For example:

    Ian ate $1\frac{1}{2}$ sandwiches and gave away $2\frac{1}{2}$ sandwiches.

8. B. For example, the shapes in A aren't all the same.

Assessment Strategy: written question
Communication

Question 6
• Model each mixed number. Sketch the model.
  a) $2\frac{2}{3}$ **b)** $3\frac{1}{6}$

1	2	3	4
• uses models and sketches of the mixed numbers that exhibit minimal clarity and accuracy, and are ineffective in communicating	• uses models and sketches of the mixed numbers that lack clarity and accuracy, though not sufficient to impede communication	• uses models and sketches of the mixed numbers that are sufficiently clear and accurate to communicate	• uses models and sketches of the mixed numbers that are clear, precise, and effective in communicating

Extra Practice and Extension

• You might assign any of the questions related to this lesson, which are cross-referenced in the chart below.

Skills Bank	Student Book p. 302, Questions 8 & 9
Chapter Review	Student Book p. 305, Question 10
Workbook	p. 96, all questions
Nelson Web Site	Visit **www.mathk8.nelson.com** and follow the links to *Nelson Mathematics 3*, Chapter 12.

Math Background

To understand and model a mixed number, students need to decide what will be used to model a whole (or in some cases, they need to determine what someone else has used to model a whole or 1). Once this has been determined, modelling the mixed number is common sense to most students. For example, if they are told that a rhombus is equal to one whole, they will be able to model two wholes with two rhombuses. They can then determine how to model a fraction of the rhombus by covering it with a variety of pattern blocks.

Another important concept that is explored in this lesson is the idea that once a model for the whole has been chosen, it must be used consistently throughout the model. If the whole is a circle, then two wholes must be represented with two circles, not a circle and a square.

At Home

• Have students make a list of situations at home or at play when they use mixed numbers. For example, they might watch a movie that lasts $1\frac{3}{4}$ hours, or they might drink $1\frac{1}{2}$ cups of milk.

Extra Support: Scaffolding Master p. 56

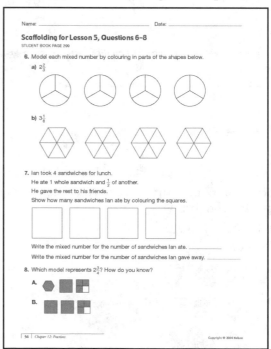

Mental Imagery: Building Fractions

Using Mental Imagery

On the board or overhead, draw a square labelled $\frac{1}{3}$ and the three squares labelled $\frac{3}{3}$ as shown on Student Book page 300. Discuss the drawings.

Sample Discourse

"How did you know that three squares would represent the whole sandbox?"
• *Because the three squares make $\frac{3}{3}$ and that makes a whole.*

"Does a shape always have to be a square, a rectangle, or a circle to be a whole?"
• *No. A shape can be a whole as long as all the parts make one whole thing.*

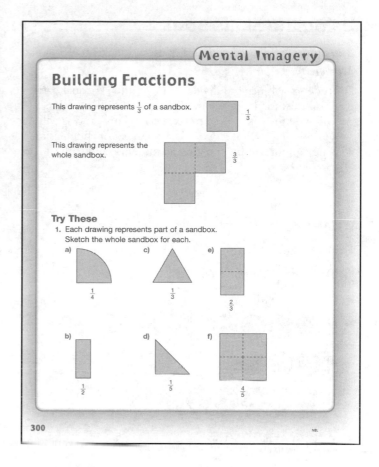

Answers

1. a) For example:

b) For example:

c) For example:

d) For example:

e) For example:

f) For example:

Skills Bank

Using the Skills Bank

Materials: 2-coloured counters, pattern blocks

Masters: Fraction Mats p. 59

7. Students will need to divide a square into six equal parts. Remind students of the modelling they did in Lesson 3 to divide the casserole into six pieces. This process will work with a square as well. The accuracy of the division is not important here as long as students colour the parts correctly.

Answers

1. a) $\frac{2}{5}$ yellow, $\frac{3}{5}$ blue

   b) $\frac{3}{9}$ red, $\frac{3}{9}$ yellow, $\frac{3}{9}$ blue

   c) $\frac{5}{9}$ red, $\frac{2}{9}$ yellow, $\frac{2}{9}$ blue

2. a)

   b)

   c)

3. a) $\frac{1}{5}$ **b)** $\frac{2}{5}$ **c)** $\frac{4}{10}$ **d)** $\frac{3}{4}$

4. a) $\frac{1}{3}$ **b)** $\frac{1}{2}$ **c)** $\frac{4}{6}$

5. For example:

6. For example:

   a) $\frac{1}{2}$ **b)** $\frac{3}{4}$ **c)** $\frac{1}{5}$

7. For example:

8. a) $1\frac{3}{6}$ **b)** $2\frac{1}{2}$ **c)** $1\frac{2}{4}$

9. a) For example:

   b) For example:

   c) For example:

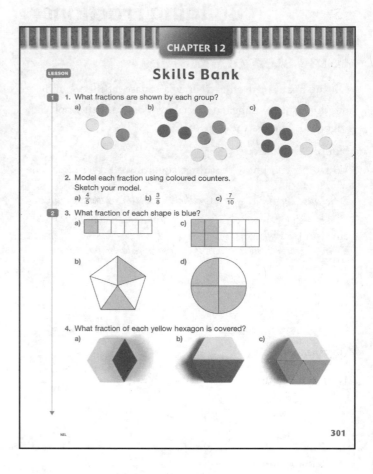

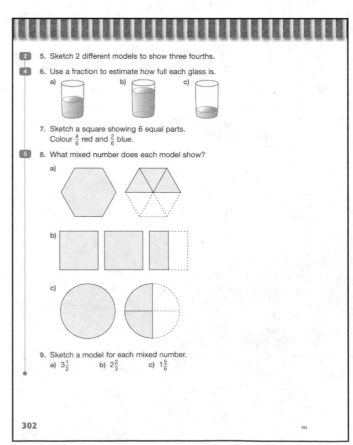

Problem Bank

Using the Problem Bank

Materials: geoboards
(optional) balance scales, large ball of clay, coins (pennies, dimes, nickels)
Masters: 2 cm Square Dot Paper, Masters Booklet p. 26, (manipulatives substitute) Play Money 1, Masters Booklet p. 28

5. The idea behind this question is that a shape can be divided into halves in many ways. In this case, it doesn't matter what shape the halves are.

6. The idea behind this question is that four equal balls would each have the same mass and would each represent $\frac{1}{4}$ of the total mass of the ball of clay.

Related Questions to Ask

Ask	Possible Response
About **Question 3:** • Did you decide to make something true about $\frac{4}{10}$ of your words before or after you wrote them? Which way would be more challenging?	• *I decided ahead of time that I would make 4 out of my 10 words start with "bu." But I think it would be more challenging to just write 10 words and then look for something that is the same about 4 of them.*
About **Question 5:** • Do the two halves of the square need to be rectangles?	• *I can't use rectangles because there is no peg in the middle of the sides.*
About **Question 6:** • Why can't you just make four balls that look equal? • How can you be sure that all of the balls have the same mass?	• *All of the balls have to have the same mass, not just look the same.* • *If I flatten the clay into a square, I can cut it into four equal parts. I can compare the mass of the quarters using a balance.*

Answers

1. For example, either $\frac{1}{5}$ or $\frac{2}{5}$ of the tall team members could be excellent dribblers. Since the tall members make up $\frac{4}{5}$ of the team and the excellent dribblers $\frac{2}{5}$, there are two answers. Either the $\frac{1}{5}$ of the team members who are not tall are excellent dribblers, and the other $\frac{1}{5}$ of excellent dribblers comes from the tall group. That makes $\frac{2}{5}$. Or none of the team members who are not tall are excellent dribblers, and all $\frac{2}{5}$ of the excellent dribblers come from the tall group, who make up $\frac{4}{5}$ of the team.

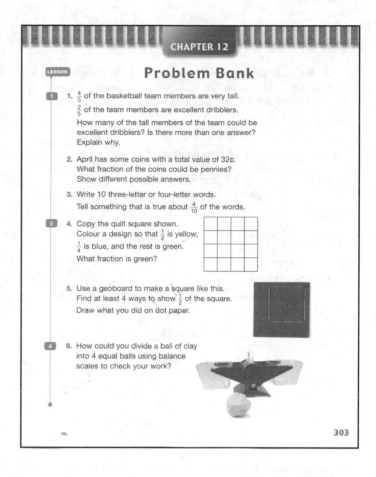

Problem Bank

1. $\frac{4}{5}$ of the basketball team members are very tall.
   $\frac{2}{5}$ of the team members are excellent dribblers.
   How many of the tall members of the team could be excellent dribblers? Is there more than one answer? Explain why.

2. April has some coins with a total value of 32¢. What fraction of the coins could be pennies? Show different possible answers.

3. Write 10 three-letter or four-letter words. Tell something that is true about $\frac{4}{10}$ of the words.

4. Copy the quilt square shown. Colour a design so that $\frac{1}{2}$ is yellow, $\frac{1}{4}$ is blue, and the rest is green. What fraction is green?

5. Use a geoboard to make a square like this. Find at least 4 ways to show $\frac{1}{2}$ of the square. Draw what you did on dot paper.

6. How could you divide a ball of clay into 4 equal balls using balance scales to check your work?

303

2. For example:
1 quarter, 1 nickel, and 2 pennies: $\frac{2}{4}$ of the coins are pennies.
1 quarter and 7 pennies: $\frac{7}{8}$ of the coins are pennies.
3 dimes and 2 pennies: $\frac{2}{5}$ of the coins are pennies.
6 nickels and 2 pennies: $\frac{2}{8}$ of the coins are pennies.
2 dimes, 2 nickels, and 2 pennies: $\frac{2}{6}$ of the coins are pennies.
32 pennies: $\frac{32}{32}$ of the coins are pennies.

3. For example, $\frac{4}{10}$ of but, buy, bug, bun, dog, cat, rug, rat, sit, and cool start with "bu."

4. $\frac{4}{16}$ (or $\frac{1}{4}$) is green. For example:

5. For example:

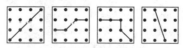

6. For example, break up the clay into two balls and put one on each side of the balance. Adjust the size of the balls until the two balls balance. Then, take each of the two balls and do the same thing with each of those since half of a half is $\frac{1}{4}$.

Chapter Review

Using the Chapter Review

Use these pages to assess students' understanding of the concepts developed in the chapter. Refer to the assessment chart on the pages 41–42 for the details of each question.

Preparation and Planning

Materials	• 2-coloured counters, paper strips • (optional) pattern blocks, ribbon
Workbook	p. 97, all questions
Masters	• Chapter 12 Test Pages 1 & 2, pp. 48–49 • Fraction Mats p. 59

Observe that students are correctly using manipulatives and drawings to model the questions.

Related Questions to Ask

Ask	Possible Response
About **Question 4 d):** • Do the sizes of the triangles matter in finding this fraction?	• No. Because 4 of the 5 triangles, or $\frac{4}{5}$, are blue. The size of the triangles doesn't matter.
About **Question 7:** • Could you divide a strip of paper into thirds any other way besides folding?	• Yes. You could measure the length of the strip in centimetres and then divide by 3 to find out how long each third should be.
About **Question 9:** • Why is folding a paper strip into fourths or eighths easier than into thirds?	• Folding a paper strip in fourths is just folding it in half exactly and then half exactly again. For eighths, you would fold once more exactly in half. For thirds, you have to guess how far to fold and try to get really close to folding the paper strip into thirds.

Journal

Ask students to write in their journals a description and a picture for each of the following:
• fractions as parts of a group
• fractions as parts of a whole
• fractions as parts of a measure
• mixed numbers

Then ask them to record their thoughts, having now completed the chapter, about the chapter goals they wrote about at the beginning of the chapter. (See Chapter Opener, Teacher's Resource page 9.) Then have them compare their responses and reflect on what they have learned.

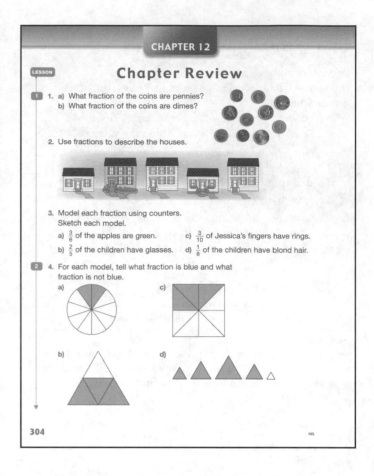

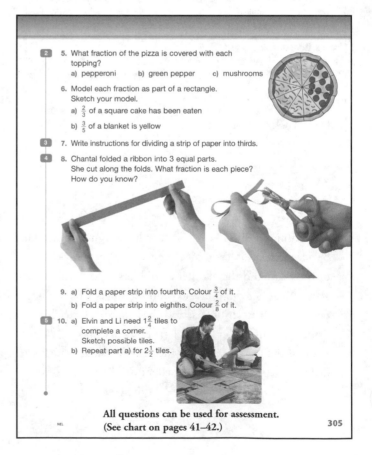

Answers

1. a) $\frac{4}{10}$ (or $\frac{2}{5}$) **b)** $\frac{2}{10}$ (or $\frac{1}{5}$)

2. For example, $\frac{3}{5}$ have two storeys, $\frac{2}{5}$ have gardens, $\frac{5}{5}$ have sidewalks, $\frac{2}{5}$ have only two windows.

3. a) For example:

b) For example:

c) For example:

d) For example:

4. a) $\frac{2}{10}$ blue; $\frac{8}{10}$ not blue   **b)** $\frac{3}{4}$ blue; $\frac{1}{4}$ not blue
  c) $\frac{3}{8}$ blue; $\frac{5}{8}$ not blue   **d)** $\frac{4}{5}$ blue; $\frac{1}{5}$ not blue

5. a) $\frac{3}{10}$ **b)** $\frac{5}{10}$ **c)** $\frac{2}{10}$

(Chapter Review Answers continued on p. 65)

Assessment of Learning—What to Look for in Student Work...

Assessment Strategy: short answer
Understanding of Concepts

Question 1
a)What fraction of the coins are pennies?
b)What fraction of the coins are dimes?
(Score correct responses out of 2.)

Assessment Strategy: written question
Communication

Question 2
• Use fractions to describe the houses.

1	2	3	4
• provides incomplete or inaccurate description that lacks clarity or logical thought, using fractions that are inaccurate	• provides partial description that exhibits some clarity, using some fractions that are accurate	• provides complete, clear, and logical description of the houses, using fractions that are accurate	• provides thorough, clear, and insightful description of the houses, using fractions that are precise

Assessment Strategy: skills demonstration, written question
Communication

Question 3
• Model each fraction using counters. Sketch each model.
  a) $\frac{3}{6}$ of the apples are green.   **c)** $\frac{3}{10}$ of Jessica's fingers have rings.
  b) $\frac{2}{5}$ of the children have glasses.   **d)** $\frac{1}{8}$ of the children have blond hair.
  (Score 1 point for each correct model, 1 point for each correct sketch, for a total of 8.)

Assessment Strategy: short answer
Understanding of Concepts

Question 4
• For each model, tell what fraction is blue and what fraction is not blue.
  (Score correct responses out of 8.)

Assessment Strategy: short answer
Understanding of Concepts

Question 5
• What fraction of the pizza is covered with each topping?
  a) pepperoni **b)** green pepper **c)** mushrooms
  (Score correct responses out of 3.)

Assessment of Learning—What to Look for in Student Work...

Assessment Strategy: short answer
Communication

Question 6
- Model each fraction as part of a rectangle. Sketch your model.
  a) $\frac{2}{3}$ of a square cake has been eaten. **b)** $\frac{3}{5}$ of a blanket is yellow.
  (Score correct responses out of 4.)

Assessment Strategy: written question
Communication

Question 7
- Write instructions for dividing a strip of paper into thirds.

1	2	3	4
• provides incomplete or inaccurate instructions that lack clarity or logical thought	• provides partial instructions that exhibit some clarity	• provides complete, clear, and logical instructions for dividing a strip of paper into thirds	• provides thorough, clear, and insightful instructions for dividing a strip of paper into thirds
• organization of written instructions is minimal and seriously impedes communication	• organization of written instructions is limited but does not seriously impede communication	• organization of written instructions is sufficient to support communication	• organization of written instructions is effective and aids communication
• uses very little mathematical language correctly	• uses some mathematical language correctly	• uses mathematical language correctly	• uses precise mathematical language

Assessment Strategy: written question
Understanding of Concepts

Question 8
- Chantal folded a ribbon in 3 equal parts. She cut along the folds. What fraction is each piece? How do you know?

1	2	3	4
• demonstrates a superficial or inaccurate understanding of fractions	• demonstrates a growing but still incomplete understanding of fractions	• demonstrates a grade-appropriate understanding of fractions	• demonstrates in-depth understanding of fractions

Assessment Strategy: skills demonstration
Problem Solving

Question 9
a) Fold a paper strip into fourths. Colour $\frac{3}{4}$ of it. **b)** Fold a paper strip into eighths. Colour $\frac{2}{8}$ of it.

1	2	3	4
Carry Out the Plan	**Carry Out the Plan**	**Carry Out the Plan**	**Carry Out the Plan**
• folding and colouring of paper strips include major errors and/or omissions	• folding and colouring of paper strips include several errors and/or omissions	• folding and colouring of paper strips is mostly correct, but there may be a few minor errors and/or omissions	• folding and colouring of paper strips include almost no errors or omissions

Assessment Strategy: written question
Problem Solving

Question 10
a) Elvin and Li need $1\frac{2}{4}$ tiles to complete a corner. Sketch possible tiles.

b) Repeat part a) for $2\frac{1}{2}$ tiles.

1	2	3	4
Make a Plan	**Make a Plan**	**Make a Plan**	**Make a Plan**
• little or no evidence of a plan	• evidence of a partial plan	• evidence of an appropriate plan	• evidence of a thorough plan
Carry Out the Plan	**Carry Out the Plan**	**Carry Out the Plan**	**Carry Out the Plan**
• uses a strategy and attempts to determine and sketch possible tiles, but does not arrive at an answer	• carries out the plan to some extent, using a strategy, and sketches some tiles	• carries out the plan by trying and adapting one or more strategies to determine and sketch appropriate tiles	• shows flexibility and insight by trying and adapting one or more strategies to determine and sketch appropriate tiles

Chapter Task

Expectations

3m3 represent common fractions [and mixed numbers] using concrete materials

3m8 solve problems and describe and explain the variety of strategies used

3m20 represent and explain common fractions, presented in real-life situations, as part of a whole, [part of a set, and part of a measure] using concrete materials and drawings

Use this task as an opportunity for performance assessment, to give you a sense of students' understanding of fractions, and to judge their experience describing fractions and using diagrams to represent fractions.

Preparation and Planning

Pacing	**5–10 min** Introducing the Chapter Task **35–50 min** Designing a Storage Closet
Masters	• Chapter 12 Task Pages 1 & 2, pp. 50–51
Enabling Activities	• Common fractions (See Getting Started.) • Fractions as parts of a whole (See Lesson 2.) • Communicating about fractions using drawings (See Lesson 3.)
Nelson Web Site	• Visit **www.mathk8.nelson.com** and follow the links to *Nelson Mathematics 3*, Chapter 12, to view samples of students' work and assessment support notes.

CHAPTER 12

Chapter Task

Designing a Storage Closet

Keiko must find spaces for her toys and games. She needs
- $\frac{1}{6}$ of the closet for toy trucks and cars
- $\frac{2}{6}$ of the closet for board games
- $\frac{3}{6}$ of the closet for other toys

? How can you use fractions to design a storage closet?

Part 1: A Closet for Keiko

A. Design a rectangular closet that fits Keiko's needs. Colour it to represent each fraction.

B. Could the closet have only 2 shelves? Explain.

C. How many shelves could the closet have? Explain.

Part 2: A Closet for You

D. Write different fractions for storing your toys.

E. Design a closet to fit your fractions.

Task Checklist
☑ Did your diagrams show equal parts?
☑ Did you explain your thinking?

Entire task is for Assessment of Learning. (See chart on next page.)

306

Introducing the Chapter Task
(Whole Class) ▶ 5–10 min

Draw students' attention to the photo on Student Book page 285. Talk about the shelves in terms of fractions: "What fraction of the shelves is for stuffed toys? What fraction of the shelves is for books?" You may want to repeat this exercise, using a similar example in the classroom.

Using the Chapter Task
(Individual) ▶ 35–50 min

Together, read all the information on Student Book page 306. Point out that the Task Checklist shows reminders about how to achieve an excellent solution. Some students may be able to work through the task as it is described on the student page; however, most will benefit from using the masters to plan and record work.

Although most closets do not have shelves on the very bottom, students will usually think of the bottom as a shelf. So they would say that the drawing below has six shelves. But some may say that it has only five shelves because the bottom is the floor. Accept both ways, as long as students can explain their answers.

While students are working, observe and/or interview individuals to see how they are interpreting and carrying out the task.

If you want to consider a different performance assessment idea, see Adapting the Task on the next page.

Category	1	2	3	4
Understanding of Concepts **Prompts A, D, & E** Depth of Understanding	• demonstrates a superficial or inaccurate understanding of fractions	• demonstrates a growing but still incomplete understanding of fractions	• demonstrates a grade-appropriate understanding of fractions	• demonstrates an in-depth understanding of fractions
Understanding of Concepts **Prompts A, D & E** Making Connections	• has difficulty connecting the concept of designing their own closet using different fractions, to the prior learning of designing Keiko's closet using given fractions	• demonstrates a limited ability to connect the concept of designing their own closet using different fractions, to the prior learning of designing Keiko's closet using given fractions	• demonstrates a growing ability to connect the concept of designing their own closet using different fractions, to the prior learning of designing Keiko's closet using given fractions	• easily connects the concept of designing their own closet using different fractions, to the prior learning of designing Keiko's closet using given fractions
Application of Procedures **Prompts A, D, & E** Applying Procedures	• makes major errors and/or omissions when designing diagrams of closets and representing fractions	• makes several errors and/or omissions when designing diagrams of closets and representing fractions	• makes only a few minor errors and/or omissions when designing diagrams of closets and representing fractions	• makes almost no errors when designing diagrams of closets and representing fractions
Communication **Prompts B & C** Explanation and justification of mathematical concepts, procedures, and problem solving	• provides an incomplete or inaccurate explanation about how many shelves the closet could have, and whether it could only have two shelves	• provides a partial explanation about how many shelves the closet could have, and whether it could only have two shelves	• provides a complete and clear explanation about how many shelves the closet could have, and whether it could only have two shelves	• provides a thorough and clear explanation about how many shelves the closet could have, and whether it could only have two shelves
Communication **Prompts A & E** Use of mathematical representations	• uses diagrams of closets that exhibit minimal clarity and accuracy and are ineffective in communicating the fractions represented	• uses diagrams of closets that lack clarity and accuracy, though not sufficient to impede communication of the fractions represented	• uses diagrams of closets that are sufficiently clear and accurate to communicate the fractions represented	• uses diagrams of closets that are clear, precise, and effective in communicating the fractions represented

Assessing Students' Work

Use the chart above as a guide for assessing students' work. To view samples of students' work at different levels, visit the Nelson Web site at **www.mathk8.nelson.com**.

Adapting the Task

You can adapt the task in the Student Book to suit the needs of students. For example:

- Use the Chapter 12 Task Pages 1 & 2, pp. 50–51.
- Allow students to explain their answers to prompts B and C orally, rather than in writing.
- Ask students to design more than one storage closet that fits Keiko's needs.

Chapter Task Masters
Pages 1 & 2, pp. 50–51

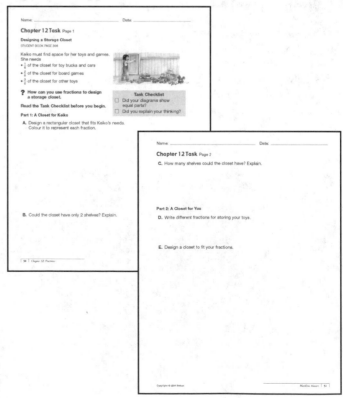

Family Newsletter

Dear Parent/Caregiver:

Over the next two weeks, your child will be working with fractions. Students will use fractions to describe parts of a group, parts of a whole, and parts of a measure. They will represent and explain fractions using drawings. They will also model and describe mixed numbers.

Throughout this time, you and your child can do some activities such as:

- Make a list of up to 10 family members your child is familiar with—aunts, uncles, cousins, grandparents. Have your child describe fractions about parts of that list. (For example, what fraction are older than 20? What fraction wear glasses? What fraction live in the same town as you?)
- Have your child make a list of the rooms in your house. He or she can then use fractions to describe the rooms. (For example, what fraction of the rooms have a closet? a bed?)
- Have your child explain to you how to cut or divide appropriate food (e.g., pizza, casseroles, cakes) into equal shares of halves, thirds, quarters, sixths, eighths, or tenths.
- Even though we deal mostly with the metric system, many recipes still use imperial measurements. Look at recipes with your child, and discuss the fractional amounts of the various ingredients.

You may want to visit the Nelson Web site at **www.mathk8.nelson.com** for more suggestions to help your child learn mathematics and develop a positive attitude toward learning mathematics, and for books that relate children's literature to patterns. Also check the Web site for links to other sites that provide online tutorials, math problems, and brainteasers.

If your child is using *Nelson Mathematics 3 Workbook*, pages 92 to 97 belong to Chapter 12. There is a page of practice questions for each of the 5 lessons in the chapter and a Test Yourself page at the end. If your child requires assistance, you can refer to the At-Home Help box on each Workbook page.

Chapter 12 Mental Math Page 1

LESSON

1

1. Use mental math to solve each problem.

a) How many teams of 4 can you make from this number of children?

b) How many days will it take to eat this bread if you eat 2 pieces of bread each day?

c) How many pennies will each of 3 children get if they share equally?

d) How many squares of chocolate will each of 2 children get if they share equally?

2

2. a) What fraction of the numbers in the grid are less than 20?

5	10
15	20

b) What fraction of the numbers in the grid are divisible by 10?

Chapter 12 Mental Math Page 2

LESSON

3 3. Write a fraction in the space to make a true statement about the spinner.

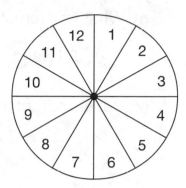

a) _____ of the numbers are odd.

b) _____ of the numbers are even.

c) _____ of the numbers are less than 4.

d) _____ of the numbers can be divided by 3.

e) _____ of the numbers can be divided by 4.

4 4. Solve each problem.

a) Sketch $\frac{1}{3}$.

b) Sketch $\frac{1}{8}$.

c) Sketch $\frac{1}{10}$.

5. a) Sketch $\frac{1}{6}$.

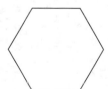

b) Sketch $\frac{1}{2}$.

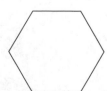

c) Sketch $\frac{1}{3}$.

Chapter 12 Test Page 1

1. **a)** What fraction of the coins are nickels? _____

   b) What fraction of the coins are pennies? _____

2. Model each fraction using counters. Sketch each model.

   a) $\frac{3}{4}$ **b)** $\frac{5}{10}$ **c)** $\frac{1}{5}$ **b)** $\frac{5}{8}$

3. What fraction of each shape is grey?

   a)

                   grey   not grey

                                   _____   _____

   b)

   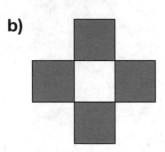

                                   _____   _____

   c)

   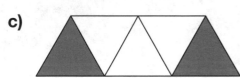

                                   _____   _____

4. Colour the model to show each fraction.

   a) $\frac{3}{4}$

   b) $\frac{1}{5}$

Chapter 12 Test Page 2

5. Explain how to fold this rectangle to show eighths.

6. a) Colour $\frac{2}{3}$ of this strip.

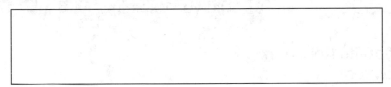

b) Colour $\frac{4}{4}$ of this strip.

7. Sketch a model to show $2\frac{1}{6}$.

Chapter 12 Task Page 1

Designing a Storage Closet

STUDENT BOOK PAGE 306

Keiko must find space for her toys and games. She needs

- $\frac{1}{6}$ of the closet for toy trucks and cars
- $\frac{2}{6}$ of the closet for board games
- $\frac{3}{6}$ of the closet for other toys

? How can you use fractions to design a storage closet.

Read the Task Checklist before you begin.

Part 1: A Closet for Keiko

A. Design a rectangular closet that fits Keiko's needs. Colour it to represent each fraction.

Task Checklist
☐ Did your diagrams show equal parts?
☐ Did you explain your thinking?

B. Could the closet have only 2 shelves? Explain.

Chapter 12 Task Page 2

C. How many shelves could the closet have? Explain.

Part 2: A Closet for You

D. Write different fractions for storing your toys.

E. Design a closet to fit your fractions.

Name: _____ Date: _____

Scaffolding for Getting Started Activity

STUDENT BOOK PAGES 286–287

A. What fraction do the plates of food show? _____

B. What fraction do the drinks show? _____

C. What fractions describe the people at the table?

How many people are at the table altogether? _____

How many people are adults? _____

_____ out of the _____ people at the table are adults.

I can show this fraction using counters.

How many people at the table are children? _____

What other fractions describe the people at the table? _____

D. What is a fraction?

E. Use counters to show $\frac{1}{4}$. Show $\frac{1}{4}$ in a different way.

F. Find examples of $\frac{1}{2}$ in the picture.

G. Use fraction pieces or counters to show $\frac{1}{2}$ in at least 3 other ways. Explain how each shows $\frac{1}{2}$.

Scaffolding for Do You Remember?

STUDENT BOOK PAGE 287

2. Colour a model to show each fraction.

a) $\frac{1}{2}$

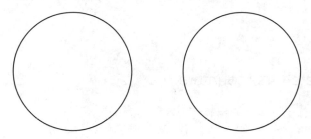

b) $\frac{1}{4}$

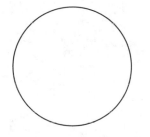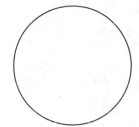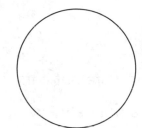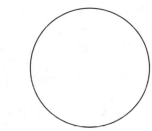

c) $\frac{3}{4}$

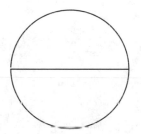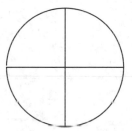

3. a) Name the 2 fractions shaded below. _____

b) Compare the 2 fractions. Which is greater?

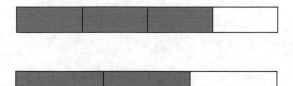

Scaffolding for Lesson 1, Questions 6 & 7

STUDENT BOOK PAGE 289

6. A kennel has 8 animals. $\frac{3}{8}$ of the animals are cats.

   a) How many counters will you need altogether to model

      the animals? _____

      How many of the animals are cats? _____

      Model the animals with counters. Sketch the counters.

   b) How many animals are not cats? _____

   c) What fraction are not cats?

      $\frac{\square}{\square}$ are not cats.

7. $\frac{3}{5}$ of a group are girls and $\frac{3}{5}$ have black hair.

   a) Represent the group using counters.

   b) How many children could be in the group? _____

   c) How many are girls? _____

      How many are boys? _____

   d) How many girls could have black hair? _____

   e) Suppose a boy with red hair joins the group.
      Represent the new group with counters and fractions.

Scaffolding for Lesson 2, Question 6

STUDENT BOOK PAGE 291

6. What fraction of the hexagon is each shape?

a)

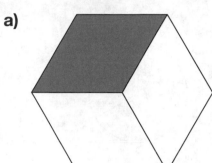

1 blue rhombus is ⬚/⬚ of a yellow hexagon.

b)

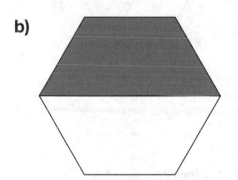

1 red trapezoid is ⬚/⬚ of a yellow hexagon.

c)

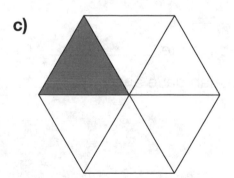

1 green triangle is ⬚/⬚ of a yellow hexagon.

Scaffolding for Lesson 5, Questions 6–8

STUDENT BOOK PAGE 299

6. Model each mixed number by colouring in parts of the shapes below.

a) $2\frac{2}{3}$

b) $3\frac{1}{6}$

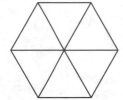 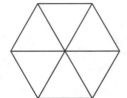 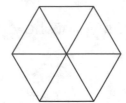 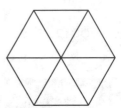

7. Ian took 4 sandwiches for lunch.

He ate 1 whole sandwich and $\frac{1}{2}$ of another.

He gave the rest to his friends.

Show how many sandwiches Ian ate by colouring the squares.

Write the mixed number for the number of sandwiches Ian ate. _____

Write the mixed number for the number of sandwiches Ian gave away. _____

8. Which model represents $2\frac{3}{4}$? How do you know?

A.

B.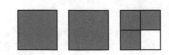

Fraction Concentration Cards Page 1

Math Game: Fraction Concentration

STUDENT BOOK PAGE 295

$\dfrac{1}{2}$	$\dfrac{1}{3}$	$\dfrac{2}{3}$	$\dfrac{2}{4}$
$\dfrac{3}{4}$	$\dfrac{3}{5}$	$\dfrac{5}{5}$	$\dfrac{4}{5}$
$\dfrac{2}{5}$	$\dfrac{4}{10}$	$\dfrac{7}{10}$	$\dfrac{9}{10}$
$\dfrac{5}{10}$	$\dfrac{2}{10}$	$\dfrac{1}{10}$	$\dfrac{1}{4}$

Fraction Concentration Cards Page 2

Name: _____   Date: _____

Fraction Mats

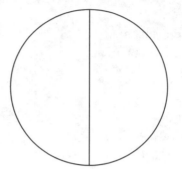 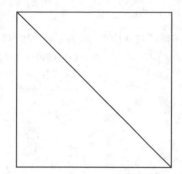 

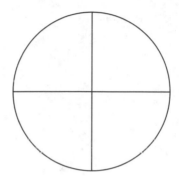 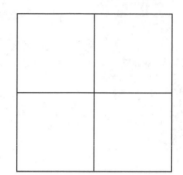 

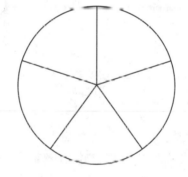  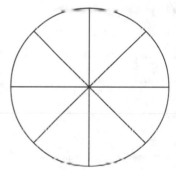 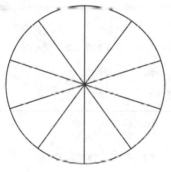

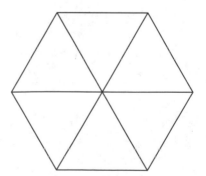 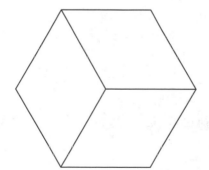 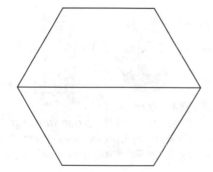

Chapter 12 Answers

Problem of the Week p. 3

1. $\frac{8}{12}$, $\frac{5}{12}$, $\frac{1}{12}$, $\frac{5}{12}$ (or $\frac{6}{12}$ if "y" is considered a vowel); $\frac{4}{12}$; $\frac{2}{12}$

2. $\frac{5}{10}$; $\frac{3}{10}$; for example, $\frac{1}{5}$ do not have an ocean for a border; for example, How many provinces have a border on Hudson Bay? How many provinces have a name beginning with a vowel?

3.

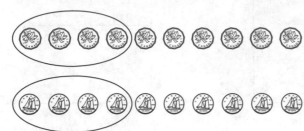

Chapter 12 Mental Math pp. 46–47

1. a) 3   b) 6   c) 5   d) 6

2. a) $\frac{3}{4}$ b) $\frac{2}{4}$ c) $\frac{4}{4}$

3. a) $\frac{6}{12}$ b) $\frac{6}{12}$ c) $\frac{3}{12}$ d) $\frac{4}{12}$ e) $\frac{3}{12}$

4. a)   b)   c)

5. a)   b)   c)

Chapter 12 Test pp. 48–49

1. a) $\frac{1}{10}$ b) $\frac{5}{10}$

2. a) ● ○ ○ ○

   b) ● ● ○ ● ○
      ● ● ○ ○ ○

   c) ○ ○ ○ ○ ●

   d) ○ ○ ○ ● ○ ● ● ● ○

3. a) $\frac{2}{3}$; $\frac{1}{3}$ b) $\frac{4}{5}$; $\frac{1}{5}$ c) $\frac{2}{5}$; $\frac{3}{5}$

4. a)   b)

5. For example:
   Step 1: Fold it across from right side to left side.
   Step 2: Fold it up and down.
   Step 3: Fold it across again.

6. a)   **b)**

 7. For example:

Chapter 12 Task pp. 50–51

Part 1

A. Answers will vary. For example:

$\frac{1}{6}$ of the closet is shown by 1 out of 6 parts of the closet.

$\frac{2}{6}$ of the closet is shown by 2 of the 6 parts of the closet.

$\frac{3}{6}$ of the closet is shown by 3 out of the 6 parts of the closet.

B. For example, the closet will need more than two shelves because it is divided into more than two parts.

C. For example, the closet could have six shelves because it is divided into six equal pieces. $\frac{1}{6}$ is for toys and trucks, so one shelf can be for toys and trucks. $\frac{2}{6}$ is for board games, so two shelves are for board games. $\frac{3}{6}$ is for other toys, so three shelves are for other toys. When you add that up, you get six shelves $(1 + 2 + 3 = 6)$.

Part 2

D. For example:

$\frac{1}{8}$ of the closet is for stuffed animals.

$\frac{3}{8}$ of the closet is for dolls and doll clothes.

$\frac{2}{8}$ of the closet is for puzzles.

$\frac{2}{8}$ of the closet is for board games.

E. For example:

Scaffolding for Getting Started Activity p. 52

A. For example, $\frac{1}{3}$, $\frac{1}{3}$, $\frac{2}{3}$.

B. For example, $\frac{1}{4}$, $\frac{2}{4}$, $\frac{3}{4}$, $\frac{4}{4}$.

C. 4; 1; 1 out of 4; $\frac{1}{4}$

3; 3 out of 4; $\frac{3}{4}$

2; 2 out of 4; $\frac{2}{4}$

D. For example, a fraction is a way of showing the number of equal parts in a whole or in a set.

E. For example:

F. For example, two of the pictures on the wall show $\frac{1}{2}$ blue.
The boy's sweater is $\frac{1}{2}$ red and $\frac{1}{2}$ blue.
One of the glasses of milk is $\frac{1}{2}$ full.

G. For example:

Scaffolding for Do You Remember? p. 53

1. C

2. a)

b)

c)

3. a) $\frac{3}{4}$ and $\frac{2}{3}$ **b)** $\frac{3}{4}$ is greater than $\frac{2}{3}$

Scaffolding for Lesson 1 p. 54

6. a) 8; 3

b) 5; $\frac{5}{8}$

7. a) For example, the three girls in the group are represented by the red counters.

b) For example, there could be five children in the group; or there could be three children and two adults; or there could be four children and one adult.

c) For example, three are girls. There could be zero, one, or two boys in the group.

d) For example, three girls could have black hair.

e) For example, the boy will be another white counter.
So now $\frac{3}{6}$ of the group are girls.

Scaffolding for Lesson 2 p. 55

6. a) $\frac{1}{3}$ b) $\frac{1}{2}$ c) $\frac{1}{6}$

Scaffolding for Lesson 5 p. 56

6. a)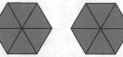

b)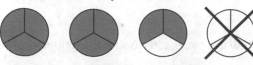

7.

$1\frac{1}{2}$; $2\frac{1}{2}$

8. **B.** For example, the shapes in A aren't all the same.

Lesson 1 Answers (continued from p. 15)

5. a) For example, three red counters and one white counter.

b) $\frac{1}{4}$

6. a) For example, three red counters and five white counters.

b) Five animals are not cats.

c) $\frac{5}{8}$

7. a) For example, the three girls in the group are represented by the red counters.

b) For example, there could be five children in the group; or three children and two adults; or four children and one adult.

c) For example, three are girls. There could be zero, one, or two boys in the group.

d) For example, three girls could have black hair; or two girls; or one girl.

e) For example, the boy will be another white counter. So now $\frac{3}{6}$ of the group are girls.

Lesson 3 Answers (continued from p. 23)

3. a) For example:

Step 1: Follow the instructions for making your pie model into fourths.
Unfold the paper.

Step 2: Turn the circle so that the folded lines look like this.

Step 3: Fold the circle in half so that the folded lines you already
have line up on top of one another.

Step 4: Fold the circle exactly in half again sideways.

Step 5: Unfold the circle and trace over the new fold lines. Now the circle is divided into eighths.
Label the sections from 1 to 8.

b) For example, the drawings were not very clear and I didn't know which way to fold.

c) For example, I could add a drawing to Step 4, and I could use arrows to show which way to fold.

4. a) For example:

Step 1: Make a rectangle to model the casserole.

Step 2: Fold the rectangle in half from top to bottom.

Step 3: Unfold the rectangle to show halves.

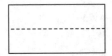

Step 4: Fold the two side edges toward the middle so that the three pieces are all about
the same width.

Step 5: Unfold the rectangle to show six parts. Each part is $\frac{1}{6}$.

c) For example, my classmate could improve his instructions by using arrows to show which
way to fold the paper.

5. a) For example:

Step 1: Use the knife to cut the cake from one corner to the corner that is opposite from it.

Step 2: Repeat cutting from another corner to the opposite corner.

Step 3: Repeat a diagonal cut for the last two corners.

Step 4: You should now have six pieces each shaped like a triangle that meet in the

middle of the cake. Each piece of cake is $\frac{1}{6}$.

b) For example, both the instructions tell how to cut something into six equal pieces.
In Question 4, the instructions tell how to cut a casserole using a paper rectangle model.
These instructions tell you how to cut a real cake shaped like a hexagon.

Chapter Review Answers (continued from p. 41)

6. a) For example:

b) For example:

7. For example:
Step 1: Take the ends of the paper strip and fold them in toward the middle until they overlap and all three pieces of folded paper are the same length.

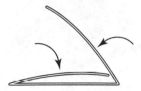

Step 2: When the pieces are equal, press the folds.

Step 3: Open the strip and draw lines where the folds are.

8. For example, $\frac{1}{3}$ because there are three equal pieces, and 1 out of 3 is $\frac{1}{3}$.

9. a) For example:

b) For example:

10. a) For example, the square shows the whole tile and the two triangles show the $\frac{2}{4}$ (or $\frac{1}{2}$).

b) For example, the two hexagons show the whole tiles and the trapezoid shows the $\frac{1}{2}$.